RUNNING IN THE DARK

A QUIRKY, SENTIMENTAL, AND LAUGHABLE ODE TO THE UPS AND DOWNS OF LIFE

BECKY HARTUNG

New York

RUNNING IN THE DARK
A QUIRKY, SENTIMENTAL, AND LAUGHABLE
ODE TO THE UPS AND DOWNS OF LIFE

© 2016 **BECKY HARTUNG**.

Published in New York, New York, by Morgan James Publishing. Morgan James and The Entrepreneurial Publisher are trademarks of Morgan James, LLC. www.MorganJamesPublishing.com

The Morgan James Speakers Group can bring authors to your live event. For more information or to book an event visit The Morgan James Speakers Group at www.TheMorganJamesSpeakersGroup.com.

A **free** eBook edition is available with the purchase of this print book.

CLEARLY PRINT YOUR NAME ABOVE IN UPPER CASE

Instructions to claim your free eBook edition:
1. Download the BitLit app for Android or iOS
2. Write your name in **UPPER CASE** on the line
3. Use the BitLit app to submit a photo
4. Download your eBook to any device

ISBN 978-1-63047-507-9 paperback
ISBN 978-1-63047-508-6 eBook
Library of Congress Control Number:
2014920851

Editors to Contribute:
Steven Morrow
Rachel Allan
Rosanne Bowman

Cover Design by:
Rachel Lopez
www.r2cdesign.com

Interior Design by:
Bonnie Bushman
The Whole Caboodle Graphic Design

In an effort to support local communities and raise awareness and funds, Morgan James Publishing donates a percentage of all book sales for the life of each book to Habitat for Humanity Peninsula and Greater Williamsburg

Get involved today, visit
www.MorganJamesBuilds.com

Habitat
for Humanity®
Peninsula and
Greater Williamsburg
Building Partner

This is dedicated to friends who have become family.

Chelsea, Britney, Tommy, Maddie, Nic,
Ashley, Andrew, Mark, and Steven:
Keep your adventures grand.

And Marcus, my neighbor.

TABLE OF CONTENTS

AWKWARD INTRODUCTIONS
A PREFACE

There are a few things we should establish before embarking on this conversation together. I like to consider myself a comedipist. It is a word I made up to explain my ability to use humor and empathy in the same dialogue. I studied the rhetorical use of humor within the field of Communication throughout my undergraduate program on the weekdays and improv in a string of little theaters on Santa Monica Boulevard during the weekends. I'm in no way licensed to give medical advice or really any advice for that matter. Including dating tips. It was throughout this time, however, that I came to the belief that studying comedy allowed me to learn something about the human soul and its ability to heal through wit, funny stories, and southern accents (I think a good southern accent will always make you giggle. Unless, of course, you are from the

South. In which case, I am sorry if I have offended you.) This book is a collection of thoughts from people smarter than me, notes written to myself in a scattered collection of notebooks throughout my bedroom, and stories from the people who helped spark light into my world. This is meant to engage in a little chat about dealing with the dark matter in our messed up and chaotic world. I hope by the end you find a few more laughs in the struggle.

One of my favorite quotes of the past year comes from an author writing about his own struggles, Jack Kerouac, in his book *On the Road,*

> "…the only people for me are the mad ones, the ones who are mad to live, mad to talk, mad to be saved, desirous of everything at the same time, the ones who never yawn or say a commonplace thing, but burn, burn, burn like fabulous yellow roman candles exploding like spiders across the stars."

The past seven years have taught me that there is beauty in vulnerability and its ability to consume, create and inspire those who deal with mental illness. I was plagued with answering the question, "Is there a place for us?" As I navigated those answers in my own life, a reoccurring theme of carefully woven redemption appeared. Is there really redemption in depression? The shame that weighed down my heart since childhood was being brought to light and needed to be unlocked and re-examined. If the Writer of the universe brings all things together for good, there must be something good to learn about our nature despite the depression we are fighting inside. There is a place for us and we belong here.

I am writing this as a person who is walking through this every day. I join the millions of voices who are broken and on a journey to understand the life given to them, one day at a time. Many of you don't know who I am, but by the end of the first few chapters you will know basically everything about me. This is one story of burning madness to see a world full of passionate people using their gifts to impact the world. Hopefully, throughout the course of this book we will share a few laughs, a few tears, and learn to love the people around us better.

There may be an important thought running through your head, which we should address now. This thought has been going through your mind since you picked this book up,

"Why did I buy this book?"

That question, along with a few others, can be purely answered by the word, *fate*. Just kidding, let's not get dramatic; I'm not actually a believer of mere coincidence. Whether this book was re-gifted from your last Christmas party, or you consciously purchased it with your hard earned money; there is a purpose for you to have this in your hands. In everything I do, I have set a personal aim to leave the audience in tears. This madness is well intended for the purpose of filling you with so much laughter that your eyes begin to water or that something inside of you moves in such a way to invoke an emotional response through the ducts in your eyes. While I have your attention for the next few hours or days depending on your reading consistency patterns, I hope that by the end of this book you are left crying. Take that as you will.

Context is important in any form of communication, so to build some relational connection points for you and me, as well as give you a little glimpse into how I title published works of writing, we should discuss the title, *Running in the Dark*. It's a play off of Bruce Springsteen's song, *Dancing in the Dark*. The song was largely formational during my college years and will be addressed in full detail later in the book. A little foreshadowing? We're not even to the first chapter, and we're off to a classic literary start.

I have never been good at piecing together some sort of formal introduction for any occasion. That is why social events have always been exceedingly overwhelming to me. I'm not sure why I thought writing a book would be any less intimidating. When I first started writing this book I intended it to be filled with sophisticated words of wisdom and deep theological sentiments. I sat down with a cup of black coffee, because adults drink that stuff, and tried to impress myself with long words that I couldn't spell and fancy phrases that sort of sounded intelligent. After a couple of months of writing, and getting relatively nowhere, I had a simple thought,

"Hey Becky, maybe you're not C.S. Lewis."

That thought changed everything.

I scratched the mellow-dramatic, spoken word-esque manuscript and started over. A choice that I hope pays off for you as the reader. I figured it was best to write something that was pleasurable to read. I don't intend for you to spend the next few days deciphering deep philosophical points with your friends at dinner. This book is barely over 100 pages — you should have it finished by the time you get off the plane.

If I was you, which is not the case, but let's role-play for a second. Maybe you're still thinking: "I don't know about this...100 pages is still a lot of pages to read." That thought is completely valid. I myself find it hard to read things that don't come with pictures or interactive games every few pages. That is the beauty of books — no one will ever know if you choose to stop reading it. A professor in college once told me that there are no bad books. There are simply books that we don't like at certain periods of our lives, but maybe, one day down the road, we will pick up the same book, and it might become one of the most treasured items on our bookshelves.

I'm going to play you again, going back to the role-play thing, and write out the next thought you're probably asking yourself,

"Why would I read this book? I don't even know who this person is." Again, you have nothing but valid arguments to stop reading all together. I am a writer and a part-time joke teller currently living in Los Angeles. Living in a city of broken hearts, it is easy to be overwhelmed with a mass sea of notable faces and the emptiness that exists within the walls of downtown buildings and lonely streets. This is a place that robs every last ounce of who you are and never apologizes for the damage. That is why my goal in life is not to achieve a level of notoriety. I heard the idea that we should use whatever platforms we are given to broadcast messages of hope. I've grown tired of this model. I don't want the platform. I want to be the person handing out tickets. To me, that is where humility begins, and the pursuit of personal aspirations looks more like a community of souls helping each other in the greatest demonstration of hope this culture has ever seen. Using music, art, business, writing, managing or the dreaded math and sciences, we are designed to serve one another.

"A life of servanthood?" Last question. Intrigued yet? If so, I've done a swell job at surviving our first awkward introduction. I hope, so far, a good impression has been left. If not, we've got a couple of pages to warm up to each other. I like to think of myself as yeast in bread. It doesn't start off great, but eventually, when it gets going, it makes the best sourdough.

Well, that's most of it, and even though I've compared myself to a fungus, I like to believe there is still some mystery or edge to me. So I'll leave this section with a hint of dignity.

With Love,
Becky

MOVING FORWARD

This might not be like any other thing you've read. This isn't a novel, a Jane Austen book, or a teen-fiction romance series. I know those are all top sellers, but I am not good at writing about any of those things.

Now, Judy Blume? Think of this book like something she would write, and then throw all of those expectations out the window. Here's what you need to know. I talk a lot. I try my absolute hardest to make a joke, and I am entirely too committed to watching every season of *The Wonder Years*.

Another tip. I get easily distracted and tend to deviate from the main point. I promise though, I will tie up the loose ends. Just give it some time.

Chapter One
HELLO

MADNESS

It might surprise you that I'm not much of a "journal-er". I own a handful of journals with the first page dedicated to how I will force myself into journaling, and the rest is filled with blank, white pages. I'm bad at following through with things. Add it to my list of issues to work on. Between a sea of empty pages, I found a few paragraphs written on nights that were painful enough to put the pen to paper. This is an excerpt on one of those nights:

"Why do I hate the very thought of myself? The thought that I'm gulping the air from someone else's lungs, someone else who is much more worthy of this oxygen than I. I know truth, but truth doesn't seem to matter in this moment. Why am I unable to feel truth? Why am I unable to feel? Would this world really be a better world without me?

These thoughts are usually followed by silence. It's a painful silence, and it comes with an apathetic stillness that hinders rational thinking and universal truth from my soul and causes my physical body to ache.

My struggle with depression and social anxiety began at an early age. It wasn't a bad home life or *child rearing*, but stemmed from the abandonment I faced after my adoption. I have been painfully shy since the start of school, and my difficulties adapting to peers left me, often times, very socially stunted. I hit my lowest point at the age of 16 when I attempted to commit suicide for the first time. After years of therapy, I began living alongside depression instead of living under depression. It is a lifelong journey that will be spent continually seeking therapy, a consistent body of loving souls, and carrying the baggage of dark nights. Depression makes living hard. I lose interest in things I was once passionate about, have difficulties controlling my emotions, and feel completely unhappy sometimes. There is still a stigma in society surrounding the issue of mental illness. People often oversimplify or misunderstand these struggles, reducing it to statements like, *"Oh, they are just sad sometimes. It's not a big deal."*

The truth is that it is a big deal. I believe it's a part of being human for some of us. The things we face in life are, in the truest sense, a "big deal." Thankfully, the art of vulnerability allows us to see one another and be there for each other in the greatest moments of life.

My notebook, filled with potential stand-up introductions, begins with the line, "There are three things you should know about me because I value honesty and vulnerability. First, if we meet and I pass you later in the day and I don't say hello, it is not because I hate you. More often than not, it is because I am afraid of you. Second, I am adopted. (This includes a few Annie jokes and maybe a heartfelt sigh from the audience). Lastly, I'm insane." The first step of conquering the madness in myself was accepting my condition. I am not like the others. The second step was learning that many others are struggling to accept their condition, too. This is a pivotal point in the human condition and invites us to share our stories. This is a chapter of my story. I hope in some way my story connects to your story.

HOW I BECAME
AFRAID OF PEOPLE

've never totally understood the meaning of the phrase, *Got You Day;* a kitschy phrase coined to reference the day a child was adopted. Maybe the phrase, *Got You,* is synonymous with the torture of being humiliated during a practical joke and that's why I take such issue with it. It could have also been the ruminants of a card writer who couldn't think of anything better for his adoption themed line of cards and created a phrase that would later go on to terrorize kids who are already dealing with abandonment issues. It's not the phrase's fault for all the kids with abandonment issues, at least not for this kid anyway.

I was born in London, Ohio on November 13th, 1991 and placed into a family at two weeks old. They officially adopted me a year and a half later making my *Got You Day,* September 3rd, 1992. My birthmother chose to have a closed adoption, so I lack many details to her personal story, but the adoption agency was able to give us a few glimpses at the time surrounding my birth.

My birthmother got pregnant by some deadbeat dude her freshman year of college. After battling the decision of adoption or abortion she decided to place me into Baptist Children's Home, an adoption agency in Northwest Ohio. She wanted her baby to have a home with a big lawn. I always knew that I was adopted because the word was used openly in our house. We had adoption birthdays, adoption related jokes, phone calls pouring in from people looking for advice on adoption. You name it, we adoptionized it.

My birthmother left a blue Bible with a note written on the first page,

"Precious one,
  I love you so very much. You are very dear to my heart. Out of love and concern for you, I have decided to place you into adoption. I really feel it's the Lord's will.
  Remember I love you,
  Your birthmom"

I've had that Bible as long as I can remember. It had the power to confuse me, overwhelm me, make me feel safe and exceedingly happy all at the same time. I was never able to connect the words 'I love you' to a real feeling. I read 'I love you', but I felt unwanted. Thus the beginnings of my spiraling struggle with abandonment. I messed up someone's plans along the way, and now I am haunted by the reality that I was and will continue to be a mistake. By the time I was four years old and ready to enter school, I already lived under the assumption that anyone who said they *loved* me would one day leave me. Love was abandonment, and I wanted nothing to do with any of it.

In my house, adoption was a perfectly acceptable way to create a family. It was easy to accept until I started school. There was something about the confusion kids were plagued with when they asked me who my *real* mom was, and I answered, Nancy Hartung (who is my mother in case you haven't caught on.) They pressed further, "But who is your *real* mom? The one that gave birth to you?" I didn't answer. I couldn't answer. I didn't know *who* she was or how to find her. If I didn't have a real mother, then maybe there was a part of me that wasn't real. I missed the boat on how to be in a real family. I tried my best, within the bounds of my six-year-old vocabulary, to describe who my parents were, but there is something in the minds of elementary students that seem to be convinced that parents are only created through a means of natural birth. Kids these days, right? Too smart for their own good.

When the other kids were fighting for spots on the teeter-totter, I was questioning the meaning of life and why we are even here in the first place. A typical daydream for many first graders, I suppose. Every recess you could find me staying tucked behind the coat of the teacher on duty. In fact, the first page of the 1997 Temple Christian yearbook has a photo of my kindergarten teacher, Mrs. Heath, on recess duty, and there I am standing right under her arm. She would usually encourage me to go find some friends or play on the swings, but I wasn't about that lifestyle. I wanted answers. I was very excited for the days that the rain kept us inside the classroom for recess because I knew this was my chance to have a real one-on-one conversation with the teacher. I'm pretty sure they hated it. I like to believe I kept them on their toes.

After all my research, by research I mean talking to teachers and figuring out how to correctly spell my name, I came to the conclusion that I wasn't like my peers. I didn't know how to interact with them. They were playing soccer and all I could think was *how could they play soccer at a time like this? There are big questions to be answered!* Let's just say this was the first indicator that I was socially underdeveloped. I felt like such a misfit. I was afraid of every person, every time I had to talk in class, and every school assembly with large groups of people. I didn't want to be seen because I knew deep down that I wasn't supposed to be alive. I was a mistake.

I never noticed the fact that I didn't have any friends until it became obvious when my birthday rolled around, and I didn't have anyone to invite. My Mother always scrambled to find one or two girls from my church to invite over (bribe) for cake. It intensified as I moved through puberty and into junior high. I got taller, chubbier, had braces, and began dealing with the frequent disruption of mild panic attacks. It wasn't until later in high school that I would partially break out of my shell and experience some of the greatest moments in my life. Those moments were also coated with some of my greatest demons.

I struggled for 16 years with the idea of being a mistake. I bottled up and masked everything in jokes that I stole from the Saturday Night Live episode I had watched the weekend before. My increasing desire for friendship would haunt me every morning when I would walk down the school hallways and feel utterly alone. It was the same year that letters filled my inbox, mailbox and locker with words reminding me of the failure that I already believed in my mind.

Maybe the world would be better without you.

That was the final letter I received before I tried to take my life in the winter of 2007. The words of others allowed a false reality to take root and create the madness screwing around in my head. It was true — no one wanted me. I scribbled out a suicide note and grabbed a scarf from behind my closet door. I wrapped it around my neck and pulled. I pulled hoping the internal pain of abandonment would leave with each tug. I pulled. Hard. Harder and harder and harder, and in confusion I collapsed because I didn't know why I wasn't feeling alive. I dropped to the floor and cried. I felt empty, abused, tortured, unsatisfied and yet peaceful. I wasn't alone in my abandonment. There are far greater things for me to experience in life than the things that I have done before. The truth is that I am loved no matter where I was born; whom I was born to, or by what means it took for me to get here. I mattered because I was here. In that moment, I was alive and I was free.

My birthmother, 19 and alone, gave one of the most selfless things a parent could ever give to their child. A family. She taught me about love. Love was sacrificial. She gave me up so that I could live. I wasn't abandoned — I was loved. I knew there was something beautifully penned in my madness narrative, and for the rest of my existence I was determined to figure it out.

I say all that to say that if you'd like to continue to refer to the day that I was adopted as *Got You Day,* then be my guest. I, however, look at September 3rd as the day that I officially became a daughter. My parents dressed me in a flowery yellow sundress, hand sewn by my Mom no doubt, and taken out to eat at our local Red Lobster. Whoever thought taking a 10 month old to eat at Red Lobster was a good idea was probably completely unaware of the fact that most babies don't eat deep fried fish. Come to think of it, it was probably a suggestion on my Dad's part. As you will soon find out in our time together, my Dad is the oddest man on the planet, but somehow manages to also be the coolest. It must be a gift.

In the years following our adoption, my brother and I were both allowed to pick where we ate for our "Adoption birthdays." This was how my parents kept the word adoption used openly in our house; and by providing delicious food as a by-product of that day, the word came with a positive connotation. Adoption was never a scary thing; it's just how our family did things. We rolled deep because we got to celebrate two birthdays, and we could try to make up some story that we were actually blood related to the Olsen twins. Well, I tried — my brother didn't care as much about the Olsen twins as I did. We were a family. A family with a big lawn.

NOT THE BRADYS
A MEMOIR OF WHY MY MOM SAID WE COULDN'T HIRE A MAID NAMED ALICE

My Mom never intended to keep me sheltered from the 90s culture that surrounded my childhood. I believe she really enjoyed the culture she grew up in, and her love of The Beatles, the Fifth Dimension, and The Lovin' Spoonful flowed into our car radio every morning and was the formation of my education on popular media. I knew much more about ABBA than Destiny's Child, and my first major celebrity crush was Davy Jones. Not the sea creature, the American/British pop star. He was the British import for NBC's television show, *The Monkees.* He was also 47 years my senior.

I stayed up late to watch Nick-at-Night every evening. I truly believed, in my seven-year-old mind, that all of the shows were newly developed series. It wasn't until my Mom informed me those shows were on when she was a kid that I first learned the magic of syndication. Out of every syndicated show they aired, *The Brady Bunch* always caught my attention.

I watched the Bradys faithfully everyday on the VHS tapes I had my Mom record for me. I collected memorabilia, made my own Cindy Brady shirts, for which I would later get made fun of at the playground (In defense of my bully, Cindy Brady shirts were a little much), and even took the time to memorize the birthdays of all the cast members. I was one dedicated little critter. If only I could be that dedicated to seemingly more important things now like schoolwork or finding a job.

Due to the synthetic reality viewing of the perfect family modeled by the Bradys, I exchanged real life with the dream to live in the posh suburb style of the Brady's house. I wanted 5 brothers and sisters who were all evenly paired with a member of the opposite sex. We would be each other's best friends, our fights would never last longer than a 30-minute time slot, and our Dad would always give us short, yet sound, fortune cookies type advice that would haunt our memories for the rest of our existence.

Being adopted made my family different, but navigating those differences was a new challenge each year. One of the hardest lessons to learn from a family you didn't look like was finding a sense of belonging. The family is the first set of characters introduced in Act I of our lives, building the tone of our social identity, the frame in which we see ourselves in the world and how we perceive the world around us.

In elementary school, girls would bring in pictures of their mothers from 3rd grade to compare how much they looked like one another. I couldn't do that. I had pictures of my mother, of course, but we did not share an ounce of DNA. There was a sense of connection my classmates were able to share with their families that did not need words, quality time, or any type of physical interaction. They were a part of a family, because they looked like one. My struggle to find my identity was something that would lead me into some of my darkest nights. Before we move forward in my identity, it is important that I give you the full context of my family. My own Bradys, so to speak.

My brother, Ricky, and I were six years apart, which meant he played the role of tough older brother, and I played the role of annoying kid sister who wanted to do everything he did. It wasn't that I particularly looked up to my brother, but he was really funny, and I thought that was very cool. I wanted to be funny too, because I also wanted to be very cool. I was loud and obnoxious so everyone could enjoy my jokes (as much as I enjoyed them), but rarely did it work. Usually, the moment ended with my brother telling me to go away. Time and time again after the rejection from my brother, I did just that.

I was always a quiet kid, I still am, because when I was quiet no one told me to go away. I retreated to the makeshift clubhouse of old paint cans and slabs of wood jammed into a storage shed in our basement that Ricky and I had made when we first moved into the house. There was a time, a very brief time, that we played in the clubhouse together. But as we got older, I played in the clubhouse and he just locked me inside of it.

Ricky moved out of the house when he was about 19. He pushed away from the highly legalistic church we were attending (something my family and I would do a few years later), and stayed with a group of friends he had met through some of our former neighbors. By the time I was 13, I was as close as you could get to being an only child while still having a sibling. I blamed myself for my brother leaving. I thought if I had been a better sister, if my family would have been bigger, or if we looked more like each other then maybe he would have stayed. Childhood in the clubhouse was lonely.

My Dad was the kind of dad that would come down and sit in the clubhouse. He faithfully sat on an old beanbag chair, while a photo of Britney Spears (Pre-*Toxic* years) hung over his head, and waited for a reply from me about how my day was going. My Dad was also a quiet man. He was — still is — a patient man. I wanted nothing to do with him.

He studied mechanical engineering at Michigan Tech in the late 70s. He barely reached his senior year because of his excessive drinking habits, but when he sat in a bar a few weeks into his last semester, he realized he needed to change some things. He jumped to different churches before settling on the faith he was raised in. He met my Mom at school through prayer, which he is hesitant to encourage due to means of romanticizing the situation. Now, allow me to explain because it is a good story and not as hokey as you might think it is heading (But warning, it's still pretty kitschy.) He was finishing up a paper in the school library when he started his conversation with God, "You let me know where she is and I'll do my best to get there." He ended his prayer (Which I may have taken a few creative liberties on reciting) before ducking out to his next class across campus. Now, context, context is everything. Northern Michigan is very cold in the winter. Students are strapped up in similar looking brown or grey wool coats and matching hats, and other parts of the face that were not covered by the previously mentioned items were wrapped up in plaid scarves. (Very stylish, very 70s, very cold.) My Dad pulled his hat over his brown hair and blended into the sea of grey coats, he looked up the sidewalk and noticed a bright orange hat in the mix of winter. We all know where this is going.

After officially meeting in their service fraternity, and a handful of rejections from my Mom later, they were married two years after my Dad graduated. My Mom said she stayed with my Dad because of his gentle nature. He never yelled. I would yell, my Mom would yell. My Dad never neglected to calmly explain his thoughts and feelings in reaction to each situation. A patience, I once hated as a kid, but now desire in my life. That posture of humility and grace would have probably gotten me out of a few life binds.

My Mom is a juxtaposition of my father. She was a bit of a worrier. I'm not sure if you have ever lived with, know of, or you yourself are a worrier — but if you can relate in any form you completely understand the situation. She shoved vitamins and herbs at us to protect us from unheard diseases that she would read in her health magazines or heard about from her therapist. Her first reaction to any situation was whatever the worst possible scenario could be for that particular event. Most of the time it was death. Here's an example:

"Mom, a few of us are going out to get milkshakes after school. Do you mind if I go?"

"That's fine. But only if you text me when you get to the restaurant. Then text me when you're back in the car. Don't text me when you're driving the car, because you'll crash and die, but do communicate with me at some point. On your way home watch the roads because there was a light mist today so the roads might be slippery and you could slide through a light and end up in a ditch. If you do end up in a ditch know that we don't have AAA so you'll just have to call the police. Now if you're knocked unconscious make sure you're wearing a coat so that you don't suffer from hypothermia while you're waiting for help to arrive. Your insurance card is in your wallet in case there is an emergency at the hospital after they cart you away in an ambulance. Other than that, have fun."

All of her worrying pushed me away, which is becoming the familial norm for my childhood. Now, before we get really sad about this chapter, allow me to reassure you that an upside is coming. As you know by now, I'm fairly long winded and cutting to the chase is not necessarily my primary means of communication. Plus, a good story isn't worth telling if it is missing the full picture. (We've already mentioned my love of context.)

Being so emotionally removed from my family it was hard to say, "I love you" for a very long time. The words terrified me because they held the weight of commitment, trust, and patience that I was unable to enter into because I didn't love where I was yet. By digging into the things that hurt, the parts that were abandoned, the scenes that were broken, I could move forward with healing and the ability to accept the love of my family. The only way to speak in love is to embrace the painful parts of the story and allow the wounds to mend into scars.

I often thought about the girls with the pictures of their moms. They defined family by pictures that fade by the time they reach their mid-life crises. My definition for family was defined by support rather than blood. It is the Dad that stays by the foot of your bed waiting for a response to how your school day was no matter how long it took for you to answer, or the Mom who claimed you the day she heard you were hers and never stopped caring about all the little things that make up who you are. It's even the brother who bullies you as a kid until you grow up and would never allow anyone to break your heart. It's the family that grows into three cool nephews and a new sister. They pick you up from countless airport visits, answer panicked phone calls, and let you tee off as many times as you need without counting them on your golf score. Whoever that looks like for you, whether you look like them or not, that is your family. Better than the Bradys. (A note to maybe revise the title of this chapter — I think I struck gold on that one.)

Chapter Two

THE OLSEN TWINS
DIDN'T PREPARE
ME FOR THIS

THE OLSEN TWINS DIDN'T PREPARE ME FOR THIS

I was a very faithful fan of the Olsen twins when I was a kid. It began with watching 'Full House' in my bathing suit and rollerblades during summer vacations and escalated over time when they released their fan club membership. I think I still have the box laying around my parent's house somewhere. They taught me a lot about growing up: how to go to London, how to juggle being a detective while being a student in school, and tips for throwing stellar themed birthday parties. Although they taught me so many life lessons, between the ages of 13 and 23, there were a handful of additional aspects of life I had to learn the hard way and not through my VHS recording of *It Takes Two*.

HIGH SCHOOL ISN'T
FOR EVERYBODY
(ESPECIALLY THE SOCIALLY AWKWARD)

The worst thing you could ever tell me was that high school would be the best time of my life. Despite my non-athletic stature, low academic standards, and obsolete social life, being a student wasn't that bad. But, if that was the best time I would ever experience, then my life was going to be one continual downward spiral into a crash and burn landing. Obviously, overly dramatic, but it was high school. What wasn't dramatic about high school?

I attended a small Christian school in Lima, Ohio. It was one of those schools where the people you met in kindergarten were the same people you graduated with thirteen years later. My class had sixteen people by the time my 2010 graduation rolled around. With a class so small, there are a handful of perks. Everyone knows your name, age, address, phone number, locker combination, class schedule, social security number, mother's maiden name, and the name of your first pet. It was really handy if you were ever unconscious in some sort of accident, maybe the one my Mom was always worried about, or if you lost your online password. Its perks were also its biggest disadvantages. Speaking of disadvantages, there are a few specific colossal ones that added to my social dysfunction.

1.) *Sports*: I'm not against sports. In fact, I played every one. What I didn't like was that my height, 5'9", created the assumption that I was to be good at all the sports. The expectation of being a good player became a load of unnecessary pressure for my uncompetitive soul to carry. I was one of the tallest girls within a span of four classes, so it was expected that I had similar talent to that of say, Michael Jordan. (He's still a relevant comparison, right?) The cold reality is I'm only semi-coordinated; I'm not really competitive;, and at the time, I was overly emotional. I wasn't terrible at volleyball. I held my own. It wasn't lack of talent the drove my coaches mad; it was my inability to compete. After every hit, block, or anything that involved my team getting a point on my behalf, I would apologize to the other team. You call it poor competitive spirit; I call it extreme displays of empathy.

"I'm sorry, I'm sorry, I'm sorry," I cried to the girl across the net. I extended my regards to the crowd and the opposing coaches. Then the whistle would blow and I found myself with a substitute. I threw in the towel on my volleyball career because my final straw was all the affirmation the team would give after a good play. I understand some define this action as good sportsmanship, but I hated attention. I was already tall; I didn't need anyone looking at me more than my height merited. We can chalk that up to poor self-esteem, but we'll get to that part later.

2.) *Social Activities:* My school didn't have prom or homecoming dances. We had a 'Banquet' in the spring semester for the junior and senior classes to attend. It was the same idea as a prom, without the dancing. Every girl spent a few hours getting her hair and makeup done before contorting herself into a dress twice the size of her body. I think it took me about 15 minutes to complete my look. With so much time left over, I ended up taking my dress off and putting it back on to add more 'prep time' to the clock. People in my school were paired up since elementary. Similar to the sports area, I also didn't fit into a romantic social mold. I never received a formal invitation to attend banquet, and I ended up paying for my own meal. There is nothing quite as paralyzing as a high school event that forces a chubby girl to buy a strapless dress and try to find someone who will sit with her at a table filled with athletic girls with Cameron Diaz arms. School was already a popularity contest. Prom, banquet, whatever it's called, seems like the icing on the cake for social anxiety.

3.) *Field Trips:* Rather, lack of field trips. Throughout elementary school I was taken to museums, historical landmarks, science centers, and state fairs to integrate the material studied in class with the outside world. Then I reached high school, and it was no longer necessary to learn outside of four cement walls painted sea foam green. I was in 2nd grade. No, I didn't care about the Neil Armstrong Museum. I was in 11th grade. Now maybe I would have been into it. There is still a chance I wouldn't, but can we at least take the risk? The only kids who ever got to go on field trips were the art kids. It seems like a biased system. You can draw? Go out! Explore! Learn. You can't draw a stick figure? Here, go clean the cheese off the Crockpot. You'll need practice for your job serving hot dogs on the street one day. *Full disclosure: none of those words were actually uttered to me. They were just what my mind assumed when I watched the art kids load up on their bus.*

I'm not sure why high school was difficult for me. Now that I think about it, I'm not sure if I've ever heard, "Man, high school was cake for me. I loved all four years." Then again, I'm sure there is someone out there who really had a swell time. Props to you, my friend. Relating to people my age was hard. I didn't want to run around on the playground. I didn't decorate my locker with photos of my "best friends," and I didn't understand why everyone was devoting their time to somehow find their way into a spot at the cool kids' table. I was focusing on other things like, but not limited to: I wonder where we'll all be if the fiscal stock market crashes like they are estimating? Why don't we make electric fences for terrorists? How come they charge more for brown eggs than white when they contain the same amount of organic nutrition? These were the questions, people! I watched the news a lot starting in fourth grade.

Things weren't that extreme. I found my niche in performing by the end of junior high. I never got cast as a lead in any of our school musicals, but that didn't stop me from making whatever part I got dynamically memorable. Even though I was given three lines, I made sure those three turned into a lofty eleven. There was no telling how many more would be added by the end of each performance. I was a director's dream…or nightmare. I don't remember what they said at the cast party. Probably nightmare. As much as I loved the musicals, it was there that my insecurities really began to come to the forefront.

People have a funny way of wearing masks to keep others out of their hearts. It is easier to keep an assortment of faces in your metaphorical backpack to use when you are confronted with conflict, love, risk, failure, or grief than to allow your red face, tear-filled eyes to be exposed. The arts are really great at finding places of healing, but when we lack honesty in ourselves, they become the perfect place to hide. Before you check out because you don't identify with the "art community," stop; you are created to create. We are all artisans in the act of shame and vulnerability. In high school, I used performing as a mask because of my shame and insecurity about the way I looked, acted, and the lack of interpersonal relationships I had in my life. It was much easier to find hope in the life of someone else than my own. I especially was drawn to the character that served as the comic relief of the show. If I could make someone laugh, I felt incredibly important. (I would later find this to be the start of my academic research on humor, but that section is another part of the book, my friends.)

At 16, I developed a personality. It's about time, right? I saved the loud and obnoxious Becky for the stage and integrated passive-aggressive uses of sarcasm into my everyday dialogue as a way to make people laugh while hiding the hurt that was in my heart. It got ugly. I read recently that sarcasm takes years off your life. High school may have dug me a very early grave. Just as things were slowly looking up, I remembered this was high school, and any high moment was usually followed by a crushing low. My crushing low came from paid postage letters addressed to my mailbox. (Paid postage is noted here because I think it is important to mention that someone actually purchased stamps to be my bully. More on that later.)

I came downstairs one morning to see an envelope with my name on it. The letters were those bubble letters that the cheerleaders seemed to master for locker signs and posters. I was envious. I still to this day have horrible penmanship. It is like a blind chicken meets an infant with their first coloring book. That's my handwriting. I digress. There was no return address on the letter, but there were a few cartoon hearts placed on the upper left corner. I never got mail from a friend before and felt excited that maybe someone was sending me an encouraging letter. If by encouraging, I meant a letter with a detailed list of my insecurities, then I got the exact letter I wanted. I tucked the envelope into my book bag and headed to school. My Mom noticed something was wrong, but didn't force anything out of me. I re-read that letter my entire drive to school. I didn't know what I was supposed to do. I didn't want to go to my parents because my Mom would cry for the next forty days. Yeah, that was an over statement.

I knocked on the office door of Johnathon Carver, who was the youth pastor of the church I attended. It was one of his students that wrote the letter, but he had no idea who could have written such a harsh letter. His search for an author turned up empty, and he apologized that he was unable to find the sender. I wasn't upset that they couldn't find who wrote the letter; I didn't want to seek revenge on anyone. I was battling what was said, not *who* said it. How do I fix myself?

I drew to the natural conclusion that everyone else must feel the same way. That personality that I developed recoiled into the shell of my elementary days. I internally, and alone, struggled with the demons of my concluding high school years. It is never good to go at things alone. I did what any good, introverted, hurt, and watched-too-many-Tony-Award-openers kid would do and took my troubles to the small stage in our high school gymnasium. Continuing to use the mask of sold out performances and bouquets of flowers after the show, I managed to cover up every emotion. I hid my shame for a very long time.

The curtain fell on our senior year musical, *The Music Man*. I rushed out on the third and final performance and grabbed the hand of my dancing partner. We bowed and stood in our place to the left of the stage as our other classmates finished their curtain calls. The high from that small rush of adrenaline and the positive buzz around the school hallways kept me going for a while. Then people stopped talking, everyone forgot the songs, and the plaque went up on the wall outside the music room. The mask was falling off my face faster than I could find a new one.

Graduation came a couple of weeks after the musical. By the time we started rehearsing for the walking order, I had already checked out of school. Granted, I have been avoiding school since kindergarten, suffering from a chronic case of *senioritis* since the age of five. It was not news to my parents that it took bribes, threats, and rewards of pizza to get me through graduation. They announced the class, all 16 of us, and I left the school building with my diploma in hand. Which to be honest is still a surprise to me, because I spent most class periods walking around with a video camera and making short films with my classmates. I didn't get pictures with a majority of my classmates because most of us were still in some type of lingering fight after being together nonstop for the past 13 years. I was ready to move on. They were too.

I'm not sure if there was anything I learned more in high school other than the importance of enduring high school. High school isn't easy. Well, except for the very few of you that I addressed earlier who had a really great time. Feel free to check out for the next few lines if that still applies to you. High school *is* an important time of your life. It didn't feel good, but it gave me some pretty tough skin. Enduring high school is the best thing a person can do. I believe in the "seasons" approach to live. Each season is important. Patiently living through each season is specifically important. Thankfully, high school is never a season that lasts forever. Like any season, there is a beginning and an end. The endings bring new beginnings. Those new beginnings, unfortunately, bring new insecurities. We grab new masks, inherit new shames, but there will always be a final curtain call.

Maybe all those hard moments during high school were the field trips they refused to take us on in high school.

THE COLLEGE YEARS

G rowing up in a very conservative Baptist church, I learned from an early age to never talk about mental health. My Mom was outspoken about her long battle with depression and was consequently dismissed from various positions of leadership at the church throughout my childhood. I watched her struggle when she was denied her voice, so I decided to spare myself the pain and never disclose my own darkness. I didn't want to be *the sad kid* that ruined everyone's recess. I wouldn't be a good leader or have the ability to foster relationships until I got my head on straight. At least, that is what Christian rhetoric told me at the time.

After high school, I applied to the film department at Huntington University. A few weeks after being accepted, I packed my things and prepared for the move to Huntington, Indiana for the Fall 2010 semester. Two weeks before I left for school, I received a phone call for a teaching engagement at a local adult program geared towards young, pregnant girls looking to finish their high school degrees. In the days following the meeting, I received thank you letters from girls who were interested in speaking with their parents and guardians about placing their child into adoption. This opened the door to follow-up engagements at schools, churches, and pregnancy centers. This led me to get cold feet about going to college, so I pulled a Runaway Bride and left freshman year at the altar.

I started traveling for series of small speaking engagements to discuss with others the story of my adoption; I opted to leave out the narrative of my depression. It seemed taboo to talk about a heavy topic with something as hopeful as adoption. As much fun as it was to take a break from school and talk with soccer Moms about their diverse families, it was probably time to get a degree in something. I wanted to push myself out West, so I didn't reapply to Huntington. I applied to a handful of schools in Southern California.

I was accepted at Biola University in La Mirada, California, but I didn't make it into the film program. Instead, I struggled through my Bachelor of Arts in Communication Studies at the private, liberal arts college. One might believe that being nestled outside the city of Los Angeles, the birthplace of cultivating new ideas, there would be an openness to talking about people's stories, but at a Christian college, it was easier to hide behind your theology classes and cynical Twitter account than talk about the pain in your heart.

During my time in college, it was hard to find people to talk to about life. Like the real parts of life; the parts of life that are filled with snotty noses and bloodshot eyes because you realize you're *twentysomething* years old and somehow are supposed to be capable of handling grief, anxiety, change, and massive life decisions while taking eighteen units of general education classes. I believe students are dying to talk about those parts of life, but society says those are signs of weakness and we're conditioned to believe that Christian college is not a place where the weak survive. This manner of life manifested into two *extreme* sides of the social breakdown of campus and one's ability to cope with hurt. There were the students who liked to believe that their parties and excessive drinking, in spite of contract, gave them a certain amount of edge, which in full disclosure maybe it did, but living in a world where pool toys were set on fire after house parties was too extreme for my introverted personality. The other option was to spend time with an eclectic group of Bible majors, who were also drinking, but this time boogie coffee that I still can't pronounce; and rereading their theology book on Calvinism for light summer reading in between semesters. Nestled somewhere between the social chaos was a bunch of *middle-of-the-road* kind of kids who were trying their best to make the world around them a little bit better than when they got here. The ones you want to be friends with because they are just good people. These people are hard to find because it takes a large deal of personal vulnerability to see them, but my journey in finding them is a major defining moment of my college experience. Here, I learned that people are mean, finding meaningful friendships is hard, dealing with anxiety at an educational institution intensifies your anxiety complexes, and sometimes, you'll find one killer teacher who changes the way you look at your life. This chapter is a reminder for the people who have forgotten what it is like to be twenty-two turning twenty-three and the feelings of hurt, victory, and growth that are experienced for the first time on a college campus.

Let's knock the hard story out at the beginning so we can find some hope by the end of the chapter. Why not tackle what social anxiety looked like at a liberal arts college first? I was sitting in the gymnasium of our morning chapel surrounded by a handful of friends, drenched in sweat because they wouldn't install air conditioning. There is nothing more vulnerable than sweating alongside 500 people while sitting on a sticky bleacher in a college gym. As the speaker continued to chat about something religious, I grew restless. The restlessness bred into darkness and all I wanted to do was die. Tough to swallow, I know, but let's keep going. This was a familiar, but distant feeling that I had not experienced since I was sixteen. I felt alone. God didn't feel real, and I wanted to go back to my dorm and end my life because it felt strongly like a logical option. After what seemed like an eternity of elapsed time, a sense of an emotional stability collided with reality, and I realized I couldn't keep quiet about this darkness stuff anymore.

The less we talk about our shame and struggle, the more power we give it. I learned that lesson as I sat in the dorms of a few close friends and told them that I was still doing this *depression thing*. I waited for the Biblical rebuttals, slamming of doors, or deeply rooted criticism, but each explanation was merely met with silence. Silence followed by a chapter in their own story. They shared their journey with their own demons, and we agreed in those moments we could never really fix each other, but we could manage our best to see one another through the bad stuff. Looking back, this was the beginning of how I saw the powerful work of vulnerability.

I began to tell my story, the whole story, to really anyone who would listen. It showed up in papers, letters, and conversations with friends, strangers, or boys who I thought were cute at coffee shops. Word of advice, don't drop such heavy issues on people when you first meet them. This is still a constant battle for me as I live out the idiom, "open book" because literally, I'm writing a book. I have a very thin veil of mystery, because here is an example of an average meeting conversation I have with strangers.

Stranger: "Hello, I'm *insert name*, it is nice to meet you.

Becky: "Nice to meet you, *insert name.* I'm Becky and I was born with a cleft in case you were wondering!"

I basically force strangers into a game of two truths and a lie without asking if they want to play in the first place. Regardless of my failed attempts to be socially adequate, I found that sharing the darkest parts of ourselves often are the parts that speak the most light into the lives of others. Humans have this strange ability to make other people feel less alone. No matter where we come from or where we go, we desire safe spaces. In our attempts to create safe spaces, we make a home. When we choose to engage the stories of other people, we open the door to their safety, their homebuilding, and as we continue to sit in the dark parts of their lives, we make a home too.

Mark Nesbitt, one of my best friends who will make his way into my story by senior year, always shared the quote, "Familiarity breeds contempt." Familiarity creeps into every relationship and has the power to destroy the mystery of humanity. The discontentment causes us to move from person to person without ever really learning the power of connection. Connection is a fancy word for how we see and interact with other people. The science of connection and our humanity of unity is where home is born. The ones who truly know us stick around because they can grow familiar without growing discontent.

I had a long falling out with a handful of friends my second year of school. By the time the fall semester ended, I was terrified to walk around on campus for fear of running into someone who hurt me. I skipped classes, only walked with friends around campus, and avoided crowded areas. My social phobia was bordering a line of paranoia, a new disorder that my brain had not yet walked through. All I could remember were the echoes of high school and letters mailed to me years before.

A few weeks before the end of the semester, I braved the walk to my car for the first time in a while and I ran into a former-friend. My heart and mind couldn't handle the unexpected run in and my hands began to shake. I picked up my pace and my heart started beating at what I could swear was an audible rate. I made it to the driver side door of my car when I felt my eyes roll to the back of my head. I blinked, but only tears fell down my cheeks. The parking lot started spinning, a white veil of dots surrounded the door handle in my thin line of sight before I collapsed in the parking lot.

You're not good enough. You've never been good enough. My own enemies treat me better than you. When you walk into a room, the life is pulled from me; you're not worth it.

Our words can create demons in others. These were the demons that filled my mind while I laid in the back seat of my car. I knew if I went home at that moment, I would do something really stupid. I'm an emotional cutter; at least that's how the therapists describe it. I feel a deep emptiness that results in the emotional decay of my self-worth. I knew tonight would be a dark one. I didn't want it to be. With every ounce of energy, I ran across the campus and down the road to the school's counseling center. I wanted to get better, and I have some responsibility in my own healing.

I called my Mom after I left my first session and told her of the rough day prior to my counseling visit. I sat outside my friend's house as I finished the phone call, not realizing the impact my tears had on my face. My face was very red. I tried to gain enough composure to walk into the house and put on my game face for the rest of the night, but my dear friend, Tommy, caught me red-handed, or red-faced if we want to be accurate.

Tommy had been with me since the first day of college. We both transferred in the spring of 2012, and met during a mandatory safety meeting. He sat by himself across the room from the other transfer students. Before the official semester began, we met in the common room for my dorm, Stewart

Hall. We talked about our rejection from the film program, living in Los Angeles, and blueprinted a dream career that would continue to be built over the next few years of school.

Tommy has a strong chin, lean stature with a slight bend at the neck from carrying a leather messenger bag filled with dusty copies of Aristotle and Henri Nouwen, and thick eyebrows that matched his dirty Irish hair. His brown eyes appeared over the rim of his round glasses with deep concern and uttered the most dreaded words for a basket case to hear, "What's wrong?"

I tried my best to play it off. I couldn't. You can't ask an emotionally insane person "What's wrong?" and not expect a flow of tears to follow. This was probably one of my most vulnerable moments of existence thus far. Crying in front of a person was new for me, but I guess that's how we get better at doing life with other people. I told him the same story as I did on the phone a few minutes earlier. Expecting some overly comforting words that would make us both feel awkward, I felt my hands tense up, because of social anxiety. A few moments later he articulated the most gracious and sympathetic words ever spoken into human existence,

"Life is hard. The door is unlocked."

We watched *Patch Adams* and ate popcorn that we had more recently learned how to make on a stovetop. Those words played over in my mind. Maybe we would all be a little different if we were the "life is hard, the door is unlocked" kind of people. We aren't mandated to fix anyone, but maybe by leaving our *doors unlocked* we enable people to feel less alone. Community builds hope. We have access to one of the great mysteries of humanity, connection, and it can become a saving grace to our suffering.

Friends come and go throughout college. Some people remain faithful throughout every hard time and make you popcorn even though you're an ugly crier. Others will build into our already impaling weaknesses and create the words that will become our biggest demons. I hope you experience both types of people. The latter teaches you the beauty of the first. This is the moment that friendship enters my story. I promise one day, friendship will enter yours too and it will make all the difference.

"OH CAPTAIN, MY CAPTAIN"

I t is important to note the time in college when I was required to take 12 units of foreign language. I was unjustifiably at my worst and most anxious during the three-week summer course. I love the idea of learning a language, but I am terrible at the execution of learning a language. My teacher, probably the worst teacher of my academic career thus far, failed me. I had never called a teacher dumb until I met my Spanish 201 teacher. I emailed her just about every morning with arguably some of the least sensitive and unfiltered opinions I've ever written to another adult. It wasn't my finest moments of maturity, but I wanted to graduate. That teacher cost me another semester of college.

In the fall of 2014, I returned for another semester of Spanish. My restless mind was carrying twenty-four units, a mother diagnosed with cancer, and the apprehension of speaking Spanish in front of other humans was crippling. On each syllabus passed out at the beginning of every semester, there is a bold printed note neatly tucked under a student services headline. It holds the e-mail and phone number to the school's Learning Center for students suffering from any physical or psychological learning disabilities. It is a note often brushed over by professors and usually brushed over by me until this particular semester. I contacted the Learning Center to see what help they offered in the classroom for students with mental disorders, but before they could speak with me, they had to have a note from a doctor. They recommended our school's counseling center or the health center for a note.

Imagine getting shot in the head three times, [somehow] walking into your campus health center to ask for assistance, and then getting put on a waiting list for three weeks. This was the frustration I found when I attempted to receive help for my disorder. There was only one psychiatrist working on campus, so students had to make appointments in advance. I was directed to a woman in Student Care who scheduled a meeting with me the following week. After our hour-long conversation, she told me that her hands were tied in the messy system of power, and there wasn't much she could do. She did, however, offer me this piece of encouragement, "I care more about your health than your Spanish grade."

The following day I dropped my Spanish class — and the ability to graduate at the end of the semester. It was both freeing and sad, but I would rather keep an ounce of sanity than graduate from college. I continued to contact the Learning

Center to see how they might help me finish my other classes, but was met with very little response. I met Karen from the Learning Center that semester, and there is a great chance that she would kick me in the shin if we were to ever meet in person. After endless e-mails with Karen that were leading nowhere, I called the Los Angeles Department of Mental Health and reported my learning disability. They promptly made me an appointment that afternoon at a clinic in Cerritos. Karen finally had her precious doctor's note and sent me my options.

"You can get a tutor!" the e-mail explained.

Those unhelpful words will haunt me on my tombstone one day. I wrote Karen a few more *distasteful* e-mails and attached a few links on mental health disorders. I was so worn out by the time the middle of the semester approached that I threw in the towel and was ready to surrender the fight.

You know the part of the story when you can't imagine anything possibly getting worse? This is that part of the story — and trust me, it gets worse. I received an e-mail with news that I had failed my writing competency exam. For those who don't know what a writing competency is or why is important, allow me to explain. It is a department wide quota that requires students to submit academic papers for review to ensure that they can write at a college-educated level. I failed, not just once, but twice.

I was thoroughly convinced I would not graduate from this college. I called every staff member, e-mailed department heads, and once again found myself leaving my corner and heading back to the fight for my education. I was overwhelmed, hysterical, and very, very tired.

The battle against failure is one of the most dangerous wars to enter into alone. We feel we are not good enough and suffer in the misery of a self-conflict that turns our minds into our biggest enemy. This battle does not require solitude, but allies who are a part of the bigger story of redemption. I realize we can never defeat failure, but we can allow failure to defeat us. We have been given the authority over failure, and we have the power to choose how it will affect us. This could start sounding like liberated optimism, but I promise this could be much more accessible if we only allowed freedom in failure. We leave the past, and the people who failed us, and walk into a place of newness. Choosing new is the greatest gift we can do for ourselves and, more importantly, for the sake of others. We must choose to not live in failure alone. My ally wore a navy, fitted pantsuit and high heels to class every morning. Oh, and she had her Ph.D. before she was 35.

I met Dr. Arianna Molloy in the spring during my junior year. She had her doctorate in *career and calling* and was passionate about seeing students fall in love with their work. She was one of the first educators that pushed my friends and me in our Communication Studies degrees. In fact, it wasn't until our junior year during her Organizational Communication class that we learned our major was Communication, not Communications with an "s." She treated us like colleagues rather than squirrels at a playground that you could throw sticks at for fun. It was no wonder that her classes had long waitlists each semester.

Molloy had long brown hair that framed her thin face. Her eyes were filled with determination and she had a confident power walk that would intimidate the entire defensive line of the Seattle Seahawks. Her weekends were packed with long hikes, kayaking, and running half marathons. She is the kind of woman that looked singleness in the eye and said, "You look fun."

She was a total babe.

It is rare to meet a woman who is driven by education, her career, and her deeply rooted passions. Girls were itching for a cup of coffee after class, and guys wanted to graduate so they could marry her already. I'm not sure if I know of one person that didn't have an academic crush on Molloy. Her well-deserved celebrity status on the small campus kept her schedule very busy, and she was hard to catch except for a glance in-between classes or a few minutes during a lecture break.

Tommy and I had our first class with Molloy our junior year. One of our first assignments was to identify a quote or motto that we chose to live by in the world of academia. I, like a pretentious fool who loved Robin Williams too much, scribbled down the infamous quote spoken by the legendary professor John Keating of Dead Poets Society.

"We don't read and write poetry because it's cute. We read and write poetry because we are members of the human race. And the human race is filled with passion…that you are here — that life exists, and identity; and that the powerful play goes on and you may contribute a verse. What will your verse be?"

Bringing a Dead Poets Society quote to an Organizational Communication class taught me a lesson much greater than a few of the sessions on quantitative data. It became a running motto for my college experience that year. It is okay that parts of our verses are coated in failure. We contributed. Perhaps failure is the key to contributing greater parts to the story.

I was lucky enough to call Molloy a friend by the time I graduated. Tommy and I conducted research studies with her as our active supervisor. I spent many of those sessions in tears while I recounted my growing sense of failure and my struggle to graduate. As I would sit in her office, drenched in my own tears, she handed me a box of tissues and sat in silence as she listened to my blubbering mess of a life. She told me stories about her own experiences, which echoed most of my undergraduate work. Molloy encouraged me to let each failure make a better opportunity for the next person.

It was cool for a professor to see you. The best professors were the ones who threw the rulebook out the window and wrote their own as they went. I recognized the grace from other professors on campus that listened to the pain of an anxious heart and worked with me so I could complete my courses. The acts of grace and understanding from these professors made the abuse from others seem much easier to carry. I was no longer fighting alone. I believe I was watching the Harry Potter movies for the first time when some discussion came up about evil always being present in the world so that the good would fully be valued. To me, those professors taught me more about life in their grace than they did in their well-organized PowerPoint presentations.

That was Molloy — a caring professor who rocked a mean pantsuit. She was my own personal John Keating whispering the truths that ideas and madness can change the world. I was able to see her after I finished my last college class (spoiler: I graduated) and give her the good, and long awaited news, of finishing my last class. She responded, "When you walk across that stage, I'm taking you out for a drink." Those, my friends, are the words that every college student hopes to hear from their mentor.

Chapter Three

WHAT THEY DON'T TELL YOU ABOUT ADULTHOOD

HUMANITY AND STORY

There seems to be this misconception that once the end of college approaches, graduating seniors instantly have an answer for the question, "What are you doing after college?" My friends typically descended into a panic attack before the entire question was even asked. Before you ask me what I will be doing with the rest of my life, allow me to tell you a few things I won't be doing after college: teaching math, working on spaceships, training dogs, spending time with chemical scientists, or being a driver for Uber. Everything not listed above is up for grabs and *that* is why I'm convinced we all need therapy after graduation.

All I knew was I liked writing, speaking, and watching marathons of *The Mindy Project*. Is there a career that integrates all of that? So far, no one is very impressed with my job applications. Towards the end of graduation, I took any odd speaking job that was offered because I wasn't really looking for money — I just wanted to make sure people felt less alone.

I started writing for the internet. I'm sure my parents are glad that is where I decided to put my expensive college degree to use. I self-published a short article about my own madness on a blog. By the way, I hate the word *blog,* and I'm looking for suggestions on a new way to frame this industry. It was one of the first times I publicly expressed my very long battle with depression and anxiety. After the post gained over 1,200 views, I found myself swimming through an inbox of e-mails filled the stories of others who felt a connection to my story after reading the online post.

One of my favorite quotes comes from the book, *Telling Secrets* by American theologian Frederick Buechner on the connection of the parallels of the human story. He writes:

> I have come to believe that by and large the human family all has the same secrets, which are both very telling and very important to tell. They are telling in the sense that they tell what is perhaps the central paradox of our condition—that what we hunger for perhaps more than anything else is to be known in our full humanness, and yet that is often just what we also fear more than anything else. It is important to tell, at least from time to time, the secret of who we truly and fully are—even if we tell it only to ourselves—because otherwise we run the risk of losing track of who we truly and fully are and little by little come to accept instead the highly edited version which we put forth in

hope that the world will find it more acceptable than the real thing. It is important to tell our secrets too because it makes it easier that way to see where we have been in our lives and where we are going. It also makes it easier for other people to tell us a secret or two of their own, and exchanges like that have a lot to do with what being a family is all about and what being human is all about.

This is one of those quotes that I wish I could have imagined myself, but if you can't beat them, then join them and share their quotes with other people. Buechner's words capture the purpose of our stories. In story, we are invited to participate in *play*, connect and interact with one another, and imagine the world the author describes with colorful words. We relate our experiences to the experiences of the protagonist and their cast of characters to engage in a story of connection. Humanity was created for connection, thrives in connection, and will only continue to exist in connection. It is why we ache with loneliness and distract our restless hearts with temporary objects that serve as only a brief reminder of the connection we long after.

Humanity and story is the apex of uncovering the truths of our souls. We learn more about the meta-narrative of God when we see traces of redemption woven into each other's stories. We are reminded of our humanity, our purpose, and the beauty of connection when we choose to invite others into our story.

It is important to share our stories.

We go through what we go through to help others get through what we went through. There is always a reason for our madness. After all my years of struggling with my crippling mental disease, my mind emitted the light of redemption. It was through story. All of the failure, fear, and brokenness can be used as gateways for the restoration of someone else.

"God doesn't remove the madness, He redeems," was the idea I used during a message I gave during a student chapel service. It might be because I wanted to drive that point home, or it may have been my speech impediment playing tricks on me. At Biola, there were multiple chapel programs available for students throughout each semester. After Dark was a student-led chapel series designed to discuss issues and topics that were culturally weighty. On Valentine's Day in 2014, I met with the student leader, Steven (who would later go on to be my first boyfriend, so I guess this part of my story was good for a lot of reasons), and his graduate advisor, Kevin. This After Dark chapel followed the suicide of a beloved art teacher on campus that happened only a few months earlier. Steven and Kevin connected me with a resource and great human being from the campus-counseling center, Michelle Willingham, who had worked with Biola at previous training seminars and events focused on mental health care.

It was important for our campus to take a night and talk about the subject of mental health. I had spoken with a few friends who were silently struggling with their own mental health, and it broke my heart to see anyone feel alone in their struggle. It was rare for the issues of depression, suicide, and anxiety to be discussed in an academic and religious institution because of the taboo nature of mental health stigmas. For some students and faculty, this service would be one of the first times the issue was even brought to their attention. For others, this was the first step of connection on their own path towards healing.

My first After Dark chapel was February 26, 2014. Steven and Kevin shaped the evening around the issue of depression and anxiety and gave me twenty-five minutes to share my story. I was sitting in my parked car behind Sutherland Auditorium scribbling out a closing thought because I'm terrible at goodbyes and didn't know how to wrap up such a heavy night. I wrote a few jokes down, but thought those might not land well. I considered ending in prayer, but between you and me, sometimes that makes me feel really awkward so I decided to skip that, too. I researched C.S. Lewis quotes, but nothing from Narnia seemed to fit quite right. It was eight o'clock and my call time to meet the After Dark team in the auditorium. I crumpled up my notes and walked in empty handed. During the worship set, I scribbled down the words, "see people."

That's what I wanted to leave the audience with because the act of seeing others transcends any other form of connection. In allowing others to feel seen — known, understood, and valued — we participate in one of the greatest postures of humility: empathy. Allow me to quote something else I wish I had written. Brené Brown is a social researcher with extensive studies on the nature of vulnerability and connection. She is also one of the most inspiring human beings on this planet. She writes, "If we can share our story with someone who responds with empathy and understanding, shame can't survive."

Stories remove shame.

The connection of "Oh, you too?" is the most powerful tool we can use in an effort to discover the light while we walk through the darkness together.

At the end of that chapel, a guy named David, who I had met a few semesters before, approached me with tears in his eyes. I gave him a hug because I honestly didn't know what else to do, and when I see a person cry my gut reaction is to go for the hug. With a cracked voice, David told me he had been having a hard time the past few weeks and that the idea of suicide had crept into his mind. I think I gave him another hug. I had Kevin and a few of the team members come sit with David in the front row of the auditorium. It is good to just sit with a person. When the last few students cleared out of the auditorium at the end of the night, I was able to catch Kevin and ask if David was able to talk with anyone who was a part of the counseling center. Kevin assured me that he got some help, and I never saw David again that semester. I did, however, think of David often and very much hoped he got the help he needed, and maybe a few more hugs from people who would listen.

The next semester, I was asked to speak at the university's annual Torrey Conference. The conference integrates academia and spiritual life. Students are given three days off from classes and are required to attend a certain amount of seminars each day. The conference theme this particular semester focused on conflict, and I was given a forty-five minute breakout session on Thursday afternoon. I shared parts of my story and spent a few minutes answering questions from the audience before I wrapped up my talk early so I could give the students a break from their full day of seminars. A few people stood in line after the session to see if we could grab coffee sometime the following week, something that has always been welcomed by me because I love coffee and people. Third in line stood David. I was eager to see him. He walked to the front, I (probably) hugged him, and he told me that he was in loving his time in therapy. We made a few jokes about being waiting room friends (because that's kind of my *bit*) and he left.

I haven't seen David since that conference, but I hope he's sharing his story. We find purpose and power in connection. Our struggles were once grounded in shame, but through story they can be the parts that allow us to flourish. I would try to write something myself again, but Brené Brown just always says it better:

Owning our story can be hard but not nearly as difficult as spending our lives running from it. Embracing our vulnerabilities is risky but not nearly as dangerous as giving up on love and belonging and joy—the experiences that make us the most vulnerable. Only when we are brave enough to explore the darkness will we discover the infinite power of our light.

LOSING YOUR MIND, BODY (MASS), & SOUL

I t's about time we discussed my waistline. Over the past twenty-three years, it has seen an array of sizes, dimensions and elastic waistbands sewn into the top of my jeans by my Mom. As a chubby junior high kid, being forced to shop in the women's clothing department takes a toll on your self-esteem — but there is nothing worse than going to a classmate's house, spilling food on your new 'mom' jeans and needing to borrow a pair of shorts from *their* mother's closet. Healing and recovery looks different for everyone. Sometimes, healing is finding a new way to handle spilling food on my pants, and sometimes it means not having pasta on my dinner plate. It can mean this scary word called therapy, sometimes just long moments surrounded in tears. It means sorrow, joy, laughter, hope that you're not alone in all those hard times, and sometimes it just means sitting with friends who also have embarrassing junior high stories.

Wounds never appear on their own; they are results of painful experiences brought on by strangers, friends, culture, and sometimes even ourselves. Wounds affect different aspects of our mind, body, and soul and require treatments that provide all-inclusive healing. We tend to isolate our healing by only paying attention to how it affects one aspect of our lives, truly believing that the extra attention will provide better long-term results. By focusing solely on the hole in our heart, we miss the throbbing pain in our arm. Our wounds require us to reflect on the trauma, embrace what has happened, and allow us to move forward as that wound begins to heal and leaves the scar of our story.

We have a responsibility to bring about healing in our lives. My weight, tipping in at a little over 220 pounds by seventeen years old, was one of the first areas I could choose to take healing into my own hands. I stopped eating bread, which if you love bread like me, was very hard to give up. By the time I went to college, I had lost 65 pounds — and continued to lose weight by picking up this weird movement called running. When I was living by myself during my senior year of college, I found myself in a dark place when I was alone in my apartment. Now, there are a bunch of scientific studies that I don't have the time to look up and cite in this book, but they discuss the connection between our physical and mental wellbeing. I started running when I needed to get outside my head — but I'm a terrible runner, to be honest. I want to be there for everyone, but if you ask me to run with you I will save both you and I the embarrassment and politely decline. I am more than happy to take you out for a nice, calm cup of coffee instead. You don't need to be good at something for it to be good for you. If nothing else, I hope that you find comfort in knowing that I make a fool of myself in select gyms across Los Angeles.

It felt good to be physically healthy. In no way was I banking on it for a career as a cover model (those dreams have been long gone due to my inability to feel comfortable in front of a camera) or a means to get a date with a boy. It was just for me — to take care of myself and allow discipline to become an active skill in my life. A skill that is very difficult to maintain, but one I need to actively pursue because carrot cake is so good and I want to eat it for every meal. I grew up in a culture that said if you look good on the outside, you will feel good on the inside — I would like to take the time to politely disagree with that belief. Although I am fully supportive of physical health, there is something very damaging about not addressing the inside.

For one reason or another — probably the influence of television on modern society — we believe the intrapersonal thoughts and feelings we experience can be fixed solely by accommodating our hair, waistline or bra size. If we are whole beings, then we must require whole healing. There is a theory called "emotional contagion." Basically, we catch feelings from one another. Our attitudes and emotions have the ability to affect the people around us. Emotions, feelings, thoughts — all those things inside your head — must be pretty powerful if they can influence those around you. That's why taking control of our healing is really crucial to our wellbeing. This is where

I suggest getting yourself into therapy as soon as you put this book down.

I remember the first time I sat down with my therapist during the sessions provided by my university. I gave her, in great detail, a look into my story and was met with a long pause. She put her notebook down and broke the silence. "I'm really surprised you decided to come to a Christian college."

I had told her of the time I was involved in a Christian youth group during high school. The organization had pure intentions to provide a safe place to talk about faith in otherwise hostile school environments, but it had morphed into a brand that determined the "who's who" of the Christian teenage community. Every student who walked through those doors had a growing ambition to be known and embraced by that group. Many times this showed itself by being selected for a lead singing role on the traveling worship team or even being picked to lead prayer after the weekly community group chapters. I, like many others, tried my best to climb the social ladder of that group. I went to meetings, attempted to become friends with the popular kids, and even tried to make videos free of charge, hoping that in some way I could feel included. After hopelessly getting nowhere and being told I wasn't *holy* enough to be on the worship team, I stepped back from pursuing a relationship with the group. I had fallen out of the good graces of the students and leaders of the group, partly due to my growing cynicism towards faith. Before graduating, I made one last ditch effort to step back into the group and try to find a place for myself. I was approached about participating in an event called, "dissection." It was designed to help students better understand how their own lives impacted the others around them. Like the organization itself, the motives for the dissection weren't manipulative. That being said, any professing psychologist would advise a better way to approach this in order to not mentally damage growing teenagers.

The student was allowed to pick up to six classmates who would openly discuss their experiences, thoughts, and opinions on the student being *dissected* while the student was required to sit, silent. There could be good stories, constructive comments, but when you're 16 — I don't know if constructive comments are ever really heard positively. I asked four classmates to come hang out, along with two parent leaders. I sat on a blue couch in the leader's living room. Everyone else made a half circle around me, and I was reminded to stay quiet while I let everyone speak. First up were two buddies of mine that were honestly confused on why they were chosen to come because they said they never really had any problems with me. They made some small talk, referenced a few of our inside jokes, and turned it over to the other half of the room. The others opened up a dialogue of all the accounts they had kept of me and in which specific ways I had hurt them over the past few years. There are no more paralyzing moments for the soul than sitting in complete, defenseless silence. I felt broken, embarrassed, and ashamed for even attempting to be friends with anyone in that room.

My therapist looked at me, blinked, and repeated again, "I'm really surprised you're here." I knew why I was there. I remember leaving that night — that weird, damaging, and embarrassing night — with complete freedom. That night taught me more about who God was than any other night of my life. I smiled at my therapist. I am not who I am loved by, but I am Who I love. I represent an echo of redemption in this broken and messy world. My mistakes and my success is not what makes me, but what makes me is the same Creator that designed the stars and the sunrise. Those who have chosen to reject me or hurt me are not their mistakes, either. We are walking miracles.

Therapy helped me embrace a lot more moments of my life that I couldn't justify as easily as the night of my dissection. Most of my therapy sessions were filled with jokes and highlights from lessons learned from watching *The Office*. It's good to talk about the things that weigh down our thoughts, because the more we talk, the less power it has over us. The cool thing about therapy is anyone can become a therapist when you learn to start listening. Many times when I'm frustrated or just feel sad and alone at night, I call my Mom. By the time the phone call is done, I feel better, I feel more understood — and I saved $75 on a therapy visit. Therapy teaches the importance of understanding your story. If there is nothing else you get from walking away from this book, I hope you understand how important every detail of your story is. The things that make us feel so weak can often lead to our most empowering moments.

My friends have become really good counselors. It is really encouraging to sit amongst people who started off as strangers and have worked their way to family. We talk about the things that normally aren't mentioned in casual small talk at the office water cooler. (Although, I'm sure with cell phones nowadays, no one probably even talks at the water cooler.) There is definitely a fine line between professional help and help from a few friends, but community is essential in healing. Never believe you are meant to heal alone. If anyone has ever spoken those words, they are very, very wrong.

Often, we allow the healing of our souls to rest in hands of someone or something else. This approach is probably why we end up feeling so empty all the time. Soul work is important in healing because it connects us to something bigger than all of us. Faith played a big part in my journey. Despite the hardships I had with the church, I knew there still must be something bigger.

My life feels like a hollowed-out tree trunk without my faith. You can still stand for a while, but eventually life knocks you down and you have no way to fight it with your mere skin and bones. Faith is a life-long journey — and if you're anything like me — there are days you are into it and some days that you aren't. It doesn't make us *less than* on days we question, doubt or become distant. Faith taught me that we are free to suffer for the greater purpose of finding ourselves in God. We no longer just exist — we live.

This world is pretty banged up, but sometimes in the rumble you find these little pieces of gold mixed into the mess. Those are glimpses of the next world.

A place where all those little gold pieces align and the sufferings we faced here, whether in your mind, body or soul, build a beautiful end to your story.

LEARNING VULNERABILITY

When I was 10 years old I went to McDonald's with my Mom after school often. So our hopping in the car to run errands and a short visit to McDonalds along the way was no surprise to me that particular weekday afternoon. My Mom ordered and I sat at the table that had a Lego board built into it, and played until she brought me my chicken nuggets. A little girl approached my table and stood silently for a few moments. I kept playing, because keeping in good fashion with my social awkwardness I believed; *she walked up to me, why do I have to say the first words?* She stared at me with a puzzled look in her eye.

"What's wrong with your face?" She asked.

Okay, where is your parent and who told you it was okay to ask those kinds of questions? I thought.

"What do you mean?" I actually replied.

"Your lip, what's wrong with your lip?" she continued.

"Oh, I was born with a cleft palate." My answer left her unsatisfied and she shuffled off with her mother to the play area. You could say that I first learned vulnerability with that little girl at McDonalds, but for the sake of writing a whole chapter — I'll give you the whole story.

A good friend, Laura Cook, compiled a book of stories for her senior project. She collected stories from a handful of people who shared the parts of their lives that once played a huge role in the insecurities and the journey they had in learning the *art* of vulnerability. She asked me to share my experience, which meant not only sharing my story, but also getting photographed. I'm okay with talking; I'm not super great on camera. I've always been insecure about my crooked smile.

It seemed fitting to share *that* story with Laura. I told her the story of the scar across my face, the scar that has been with me since the day I was born, and how the journey to find the meaning of it became a lifelong struggle. I don't want to ruin Laura's book, but my scar was once one of my biggest insecurities and is slowly working itself to becoming a physical form of my ability to be vulnerable.

The typical response from those who chime in about halfway through my story is, "The doctors did a really good job. I can hardly tell you ever had a cleft lip." I appreciate their kind remarks, but no matter how nice the words can be — there is no way to negate the impact having a crooked face has on a little girl's self-esteem. Their words, by the age of 5, already became numb in my mind, because the mirror always told a different story.

I guess you can say my cleft lip has been my oldest *frenemy* since it was there for me during my (probably) painful birthing experience, and the reason I had to wear a fake tooth in my retainer for most of high school. It was first repaired when I was two months old, and corrected over the next 20 years as I grew into my skin and deviated septum. It is always very heartening to know that people say they don't notice anything at first, but once you've been told about the scar, you'll always notice. There has been plenty of money placed into my face, and let me tell you — it's a very average face. No amount of money could fully take that scar away. Perhaps that's the real beauty of scars, they can never be fully removed from their stories.

Over the years, and struggles to accept it, the scar has become a permanent resident on my lip for little girls at McDonalds to point out while I'm playing with Legos. Luckily, over much time, I've learned that my scar becomes a part of who I am — just as much as the sound of my laugh or the monotone timbre in my voice.

My scar reminds me of the fragility of life. It reminds me that casting agents may never cast me as an understudy for Emma Watson, but I'm still in Precious hands. My scar showed me the real meaning of healing, of vulnerability. There is great power in our scars. Our scars tell our stories. I hope you fall in love with your scars because they will become your story. We have to learn to love our stories. The better we get at being us, the better we get at being with others.

While I was preparing to speak at an event, I grabbed coffee with a handful of people to get their thoughts on different topics. I was drawn to the idea of talking about society and where in the world we fit in. The dominant trait I noticed as I sat down with people and learned more about their own stories was the biggest issue people had with society was often the same issue they struggled with in their own life. Many friends shared their struggles of eating disorders, and in the same heartbeat, shared their disgust with the beauty standards on billboards down Sunset Boulevard. Another friend was grappling with religion and philosophy, but had no interest in walking back into the church because he hated the idea of "big businesses" and just being rich for the sake of being rich. There was always validity to their hurts and concerns, but I saw a richer transaction between their scars and their stories. We can never eradicate the images given to us, but we have every choice in how we will let them influence the way we see ourselves.

Steven is a sociology major and has attempted to teach me the textbook definition of 'society' multiple times, but to his eye-roll, I like to see it as "a bunch of people hanging out and doing life" (Don't ever use that as a quote in an academic paper, because you will fail). To appease Steven and his summa-cum-laude—earning education, I've looked up the academic definition of society. Society is similar to the definition of culture in that it offers one of the greatest paradoxes in the history of man. We control what society looks like, but society controls what we look like. It's confusing and tricky, but allow me to break it down this way. We have a say in what society says to us, but only if we see brokenness in society and tend to the wound. All that stuff we see that we are sick of dealing with is largely society reporting the stories of our wounds, not our scars. Because, darling, our wounds are worn on ourselves for everyone to see, but rarely do we see the beauty of our scars. We keep them covered in good fashion to save the awaiting embracement that comes with a past. Although it's been shared time and time before, and you are very smart and educated so you may not need to hear it again, I'm going to make you read it anyway: everyone has a past and everyone has a few scars. Scars are the dirty stories filled with tears, victory, triumphs, hurdles, and every other important sport expression that could be inserted into this sentence.

There is a theory researched by Walter Fisher called Narrative Paradigm. The crux of his theory says we are storytellers by nature. We exist, breathe, relate, and understand through a lens of story. We get lost in society because society has a megaphone, shouting our wounds, and we've learned to accept *that* story as true. In Narrative Paradigm, Fisher attached an idea called Narrative Fidelity which he says causes us to accept the stories that match our existing beliefs. That means, to modify a line from one of my favorite novels *Perks of Being a Wallflower*, we accept the messages we think we deserve.

I was sitting in the garage of Tommy's house during one of our final semesters of college. We were both sitting on the edge of some broken relationships, and received too many *no's* from too many people that should have said *yes*. Tommy was sent out on auditions that were solely measured by the way he looked, walked, and sometimes even his tone of voice. (Which is roughly a deep baritone if anyone wanted to know.) Being surrounded in a world that told him only his looks would get him a job, he was caught in a whirlwind of self-doubt. Self-doubt that looked very similar to my own, but that was impossible because he was a good looking dude who too many girls wanted to date, and I was a chubby, white girl with dark roots and a crooked smile so there was no way he could know what it's like to hate the way you look. All I wanted was a normal smile. He had exactly what I wanted: a normal lip.

Tommy turned his tall, black desk chair away from his computer filled with instrumental loops and Mat Kearney albums, and took a drink from his IPA.

"Sometimes I just wish I was in an accident and got a huge scar across my face."

I guess the saying, *the grass is always greener*, holds up. Tommy took another sip of his beer and turned back to his computer screen. I was lost in his statement. I had never disclosed my insecurity about my own scar with Tommy. I never told him what is was like to live a life with a huge scar across your face, and how painful and disappointing life can be sometimes because of it.

He was tired of being worth only his appearance, a belief we shared, but we stood on two opposite sides of the spectrum. Why does this stuff have to matter? Why do some kids have to be born with messed up faces and why are some expected to excel because they look good in yearbook pictures? There we sat, two broken little pieces, who struggled to get jobs, dates, good grades, etc. I wish I had a great answer. I wish I could tell you that Tommy and I left that night with the perfect answer to tell your friends that are walking through the same thing. Maybe that's the point. There is no answer to why we are the ones who have to suffer with the wounds we have, but we are not alone. For a long time, I blamed the scar across my face for the reason why I wasn't connected. I will never be *pretty* like the other girls. I will never know the feeling of real front teeth, or life without a lazy eye created by all the early skin grafts.

That night Tommy shattered everything I knew about society's beauty standard. We were the ones creating what society said about us. Perceptions matter, don't get me wrong, but the way we perceive ourselves and our experiences is far greater than what a broken world says about us. We're all outsiders looking for connectedness. If you ever meet anyone who seems to be *on the inside* call me and let me know and I'll append this chapter. We all have deep cuts in us — physical, internal, self-inflicted, born-with, created by others. We're all pretty banged up. Some of us have gotten really good at smothering the redness with concealer. We've suppressed those scars so we never have to allow ourselves to feel weak; we never want to feel weak.

Walk around with a scar across your face (How many more times do you think I can use that phrase in this chapter?) and it'll teach you quickly that there is nothing you can do but surrender the perceptions of *weakness* and allow for something beautiful to happen.

My lip serves as a reminder to the story of victory. As much as my physical scar became a part of my character, so do my internal ones, the ones that no one sees. All of it is my story. We lose the ability to connect with people the longer we hide our scars. By uncovering all of these hidden parts of us, we finally experience redemption. Redemption is not starting over, but reclaiming what was already there for good. Vulnerability allows our scars to serve as stories and reclaim the shame they once served us. My scar helped me see the scars of others. If we start to talk about our scars, people will feel seen in their wounds. Sometimes, I can't drink out of water bottles correctly and water splashes down the side of my face; and my slurred speech will show up the longer you get to know me, but battle wounds are where the good stories are — and I'm all about a good story.

Allow me to speak this into our society in order to reverse the effects of this perception of scars. Scars are beautiful. They are the strongest thing about us, because we are resilient creatures designed to overcome barriers and odds. We are the only living beings that can truly love another person and that is remarkable. Scars teach us to love, they teach us to see, they teach us that we heal.

"YOU'RE FUNNY, KID"

owned a handful of Saturday Night Live *Best Of* compilation disks as a kid that I watched over and over with my friends during our weekends. Growing up in such a small town, there were few options to keep yourself entertained, so you had to figure out ways to keep away from sex and drugs and going to the local corn maze again. My friends and I decided to watch Jimmy Fallon in everything he was in and copied every voice Amy Poehler ever used in a sketch. I saved up money to buy a video camera, scooped up wigs from the discount table of every Halloween store in town, and started filming my friends during study halls. We made some pretty awesome stuff, but I will take those videos with me to my grave.

It came as no surprise to my parents when I told them I was looking into improv classes shortly after moving to Los Angeles. I found cheap classes online and by the next week was enrolled in an 8-week introductory course in performing long-form improv. The classes were held in an old building on Santa Monica Boulevard that was used as a hub for casting agents looking for extras in their B-list films. After two initial attempts to find the entrance, a stranger tapped me on the shoulder and informed me that he found an open door further down. We walked in to the dusty building and poked our heads into every open room, trying to find the classroom. We settled on a room with a small stage and two rows of broken theater-style seats — call it intuition or the small sign marked on the wooden door, Improv LA. We waited a few minutes for everyone to arrive, the teacher was arranging his things. I thought about leaving as each moment dragged on, and fellow students tried their best at making a good first impression by supplying a satirical comment on *how bad traffic was outside.* It's Los Angeles. We've heard the traffic jokes — every one — they are never funny.

The twelve of us sat in a small room with a broken air-condition and were instructed to share our first improv experience. I wiped the sweat off my eyebrows, because I seem to collect an awful lot of perspiration up there —and began a non-verbal debate in my head whether to just buy into the room and get an easy pity laugh by making a joke or if I should just play it cool and mysterious—"I TOOK A CLASS AT 16!"

I couldn't even play it cool for like four seconds before that blurted from my mouth. Sometimes, I have this problem where I say too much in spaces that have not been socially allotted a large amount of soapbox time. It got me in trouble in junior high while I was asking to use the restroom, but also in this moment. "My first improv experience was probably my audition for my school play my seventh grade year. Those things are like one big improv mess, am I right?" I guess I was going to go with making a joke for introduction to the group. No one laughed. Neither did I, and I sank into the back of the broken chair.

Some of my first improv experiences really were during my school musicals. Namely, because I was never given a part in the musical, so I always made up my own script. Year after year I would stand in front of the judges sporting a middle-part matted by my grease-strung bangs that illuminated like the braces around my teeth. My acne was in pre-pubescent stage, just enough to look gross, but not enough for a lethargic Becky to run upstairs and grab a cover up stick. I sang a mouse-y rendition of the "Star-Spangled Banner" because that was one of the only songs I knew by heart. By the time I reached *land of the free* I could see the director look at the call sheet to see how many more of these auditions they would have to sit through today. I ended my song and stood in silence while the choir teacher nodded his head and gave a rehearsed, "well done." The call list sheet was posted the next day and my name was (properly) listed in the chorus section. If you know nothing about theater language in high school, "chorus" was actually code for: "Hey bud, you were so close. Actually, not close at all, but we need some people to stand in the background and your Mom reassured us you could do that."

After seeing my name on that chorus sheet, I was determined to get a part by the time I finished high school — I didn't need a leading lady or anything because I'm not that kind of girl, but just the funny sidekick was all I really wanted. To ensure a better audition the next year, I studied at an acting studio in Toledo, Ohio the following summer. The woman who ran the studio tucked me under her wing and trained me in the basics of audition skills in order to be sent out to Los Angeles during pilot season. I really just wanted that minor lead in my school musical. By the time pilot season rolled around, I had to make the decision whether to stay in school or move to Los Angeles. I decided to stay in high school because I was very committed to appeasing 7th grade Becky's dreams of landing a role in the musical, and my parents didn't really want to live in LA.

In my high school it was a big deal if you had a part in the school musical because we were pretty good. I started building my musical resume, and it looked a little something like this: 8th grade —chorus, 9th grade — chorus, 10th grade — chorus, 11th grade — didn't have a musical, 12th grade —12th grade was my year, and then I got chorus. I didn't get the part of *The Mayor's Wife* in Meredith Wilson's *The Music Man*, but what I did get was Ethel Toffelmier, the pianola girl — one of the mayor's wife's best gal pals. Ethel had three lines; three lines the directors felt needed a microphone. I felt like Meredith's script was very well put together, but lacked in character development for Ethel, and she really deserved some more screen time. I thought those three lines might sound better as a lofty twelve — teaching me my first lesson of improv.

Fast forward three years and one sketch writing class at UCB later, I found myself stuttering through my introduction at my first improv class. Eight weeks later, my improv level 1 group put on our first improv show at a small theater on Santa Monica Boulevard. I didn't step out of the backline often, but when I did, the audience laughed and I was hooked. I always knew there was something beautiful about humor, but I couldn't explain it — it was just an experience that happens in rare moments between friends or on a stage in front of 25 people.

I really started doing research on the use of humor in Communication Studies my senior year of college because I needed an excuse to explain my excessive viewing of NBC's *The Office*. I stumbled on a book about the psychology of humor at a bookshop in Pasadena and brought it to Molloy the next day. I read to her a few sections that stuck out to me and rattled off the basic rules of improv. It has been said before that studying humor too much causes us to lose the mystery and beauty of comedy. With that being said, there was still a space to understanding humor and connection. Humor engages our ability to play with one another, a trait that I believe is becoming a rarity in our social network driven society, a society that I am often very guilty of hiding behind. While on an annual family vacation to Orlando, Florida I learned from my 6-month old nephew, Hunter, how uniquely we are wired to use humor in communication. Hunter couldn't speak a single word, but I tried to make him laugh. I mean I would spend so much time on the floor with him trying to even get a smile to crack across his face. The moment he giggled was the moment I felt like he heard me and I got through to him. In my three years of improve, I learned the very few rules to create an improv scene:

1. Never say no.
2. Listen to your partner.

RULE #1: NEVER SAY NO

This rule could also be translated as "yes, and…" By using this language, we are able to build a scene because we eliminate the word "no" from our imaginary space. I had gotten to know a barista in the Arts District of downtown Los Angeles who was 6'7". He told me that nearly every day he heard a joke about how tall he was: *how's the weather up there?* I asked him if those jokes ever bothered him, and he said they didn't even though he heard them a hundred times a day. He told me that the moment he denied someone of that joke and shut them down because it wasn't clever is the moment he denied them a moment of connection. They are just trying to play because we are humans, and we desire to be connected and sometimes that means we make jokes about tall people and the weather. By denying someone in our language, we deny them a piece of their humanity. Although there are healthy times to exercise the word "no" in our lives, by continually denying others — we are denying their humanity. Our insecurities are associated with our social behaviors and when a person is told *no* whether it's through friends, coworkers, the media, or by strangers at a coffee shop, we tend to shut down and it leads us to stop trying. The *yes and* rules teaches us that humanity is not merely recognizing a person's idea, but also contributing. Going back to this Facebook driven universe we live in — we are wired to believe that by simply looking through pictures on social media we are connected to someone.

RULE #2: LISTEN TO YOUR PARTNER

It takes two people to play and that is why the rule to listen is crucial to building an improv scene. It would be really lame if your sketched bombed solely based on the fact that you weren't listening to your partner, and you were mindlessly wandering through your own world trying to steal the spotlight. Listening is a humility tool that I am still slowly attempting to make more important in my life. I am terrible at listening. It's not because I don't care —I warn Steven before we watch a movie that I might cry if it involves any type of social justice, ie: *The Help*. I am so quick to jump in with a rebuttal or comment on whatever is being said that I often miss the beauty of the conversation. Listening teaches us empathy — a skill set uniquely found in understanding our use of humor. We suspend our experiences and biases for just a moment and allow the joy or pain of someone else to step into our shoes.

I started a pilot study my junior year of college that focused on the impact humor has on our ability to relate and connect to others. The questions that surrounded the 30-minute interview were largely focused on the interviewee's experience with their interpersonal relationships and how they used humor on a daily basis. Here are a couple of my favorite quotes from those interviews:

> "Humor moves from initiated relationships to enjoyment of relationship. It's not long turning it into relational energy, but you are laughing because out of enjoyment of the other person."

"My friends are pretty funny too. They make me laugh, for the most part. The best ones are the ones that make me laugh most. I don't know if that's because they are funny or because I love them so much. There's no sense of humoring people you love so much, there's no a 'I'm going to laugh to make him feel better.' These people that make you laugh so much they wouldn't have to do anything to make you laugh."

"This sounds morbid, but we say, "If you don't laugh, you'll kill yourself." For those times that if you can't laugh about this right now and see it for the absurdity that it is, we're going to jump off a bridge. I think humor can be used as a means to not actually deal with the issues at hand, but I think we use it in a way that gives us courage to face the issues at hand. The ability to laugh at it reminds us that we can beat it. We can wrestle with it. We still have power and agency over it."

"Humor allows us to be brave."

Humor is one of my favorite things to talk about because I believe there is something really powerful in using humor to bring about healing. Humor is influential in building bridges in relationships while finding room to express ourselves along the way. Bravery and freedom can be accessed through something so simple as sharing a laugh with a complete stranger. It reminds us we were never designed to be alone. Humor allowed me to talk about the hard stuff for the first time and begin the path of my own healing. If I could laugh with someone about it, I found I could offer a place to invite someone into my story and create a space for empathy.

Empathy is not just hearing the story of another person (See improv rule #2), but having the courage to step inside the story and contribute to the ending (see improv rule #1). We've gotten really bad at listening to each other, and we're always running around trying to use our own agenda to get others to do what we want them to do —but in all honesty, life is just one big sketch that we are making up along the way. In order to give this world the best we've got, we must listen and we must contribute.

SOCIAL LIFE OF AN INFJ

Does anyone have a year of their life that was by far the worst year? 2001. I'm mean there were a lot of terrible things happening globally that made this year terrible, and as a 4th grader battling her first round of pimples —it made it much tougher. The 10 extra pounds that found me over summer forced me to wear a size larger of my blue and green uniform skirt; the tub that held all my Mary-Kate and Ashley books broke in half, and I would later bet this was the year that I became significantly less intelligent. I blame all the cursive they made us do for every assignment —it was far too distracting to focus on anything else if the teacher would fail you for writing the cursive capital 'Z' wrong. In all honesty, I'm still not sure. This was the first year that truly documented my journey as a social wallflower.

All the girls in my class got invited to a cool birthday party. *All the girls* except one. You guessed it —me. I was rarely invited to parties or really had parties for that matter, so I didn't realize that not being invited was an odd occurrence. One day when the weather was bad outside, and we were forced to play inside for recess (which was my favorite because I got to sit in the corner and read my books). Across from my corner, the other girls sat on the bench of the piano that was located in our classroom. They were spread around the girl who was throwing the birthday party — let's call her, Lisa.

Lisa and the girls were going over the birthday party agenda. Intrigued by all the fun-sounding party plans, I moved a little closer to hear the conversation by pretending to swap out my Nancy Drew novel for another from my broken tub. I guess all those teenage detective novels I was reading worked well. I sat back in my corner and continued to read — but with one eye peering over the top of my book, so I could keep a good view on what was happening.

Lisa began to walk over to me. I'm sure she must have spotted me spying —I was toast. I threw my head down and glued my eyes to the words on the page. *Maybe she didn't see, maybe she didn't see. Oh no, are my hands clammy? THIS WAS A PAPERBACK TOO!*

"Hi."

Do I shake her hand? I mean I've known her since kindergarten.

"Hi." I said.

Lisa handed me a piece of paper and I opened it to find an invitation. *Okay, Becky, play it cool.*

"Oh, what's this? *Good, Becky, that was really good."*

"Someone else can't come. So you can come," Lisa replied to my wide-eyed gaze. She walked back to her entourage of 4th grade girls and I tucked the paper into my book.

All I'm going to say is I went to that party and it was a *very* fun time. It wasn't until years later, like most of the things I've expressed in therapy, that I remembered sitting in the corner watching all the girls giggle about all the things they were going to do. It was those few moments that created so much shame and shaped how I viewed myself within community.

What was wrong with me?

This question has followed me like a bad movie tagline for the past few years, and is still one that I often work on silencing every day. I felt like a kid at camp who missed the first day because my parent's car broke down along the way, and I didn't make it in time for the first bonfire meeting. All the other kids are having this great time and have somehow managed to go from complete strangers to best friends over the course of six hours — but it never felt like there would be room for me. I was always surrounded by people, but I was never a part of community. I know I was not the only one battling the desire to find a place to call home. I wanted to write something for the kids who have felt inadequate for far too long because their story feels lost in the noise.

Have you ever heard of the Meyers-Briggs personality test? If you have, feel free to skim down about four more lines while I take the time to explain to our friends about the personality test. Ask any graduating senior from a standard university about their Meyers-Briggs results, and they will probably give you four letters that don't spell a word. Each letter points out a specific personality trait that is custom built in us that explains how we perceive and interact with the working world. There are 16 different configurations, and I proudly am the rarest type: INFJ: introverted, intuition, feeling, and judging. These are four feelings that have made me feel alone, broken, and unimportant. For a very long time, I felt like my story was missing because I wasn't like the other extroverted people in my life. Even the other introverts — they dressed cool and were really talented artists. I didn't even feel like I fit into a standard personality test. They list online popular people who have similar personality types as you, and I'm pretty sure I was a similar match to Gandhi. I guess that's fine, but what I really wanted was someone from the cast of *Good Will Hunting* or maybe *Boy Meets World*.

Maybe it's a remnant of my personality type or the result of being incredibly shy that caused me to feel so disconnected from other people. Dealing with darkness probably didn't help attract any potential suitors (and my suitors, I just mean friends.) Sometimes when all the clutter, which includes, but is not limited to: your struggles, your experiences, and the way you are wired, builds itself so high inside your head sometimes the only thing you can trust is the fact that *you* are the problem.

I'm here to tell you — you are *not* the problem.

So how do we move forward? People.

Get your awkward self away from the punch bowl and find someone to talk to when you're at that school dance. The way we think about ourselves is largely influenced by the voices of the people we keep in our hearts. People are really important. Who we choose to call *friend* in this life should not be taken lightly. True friendship gives us glimpses of the next world and the perfect love we were designed to receive and give. I've chosen in my short-lived 23 years that I don't want to surround myself with people who don't invite me to their birthday party. Voices are powerful because they can create the most satisfying affirmation a human will ever know, or spark the greatest demons a human will ever fight.

Sometimes I hate myself. If this book is about honesty, then it is important that you know it. Sometimes I surround myself with people who don't like me either, because in some sick, twisted way I want someone else to hate me as much as I hate myself. There have been moments that I wished the people who love me hated me.

Who even does that?

Me. Insecure me who chose a lot of wrong voices for too many years. As much as I try to fight with myself on the subject, I know it is best to find the *unconditionals*.

We are need unconditionals. They are the kind of friends that whisper words of love into my little INFJ ears that want nothing more than to keep parts of my heart to myself. The connection of *no questions asked* is a small glance of humanity being restored to its Creator who always says, "No questions. I love you."

The greatest connections I've made with people begin with the words, "I've never told anyone this before…" I think because I hear those words as an invitation to becoming someone's unconditional. We were not put on this earth to live as conditional people with conditional friendships and a conditional faith. By breaking down the walls of conditional, we all get an invite to the birthday party — not just because someone else couldn't go. I need the unconditionals in my life to point me to the truth that I am unconditionally loved no matter my darkness.

I dare you to find your unconditionals and give them a call, e-mail, text, or tweet and tell them, "Thank you." I then triple-dog dare you to commit to being an unconditional human being in the way you treat others. Smile at a stranger, answer the phone at 3 AM, or just leave a generous tip for your busy waitress. Be an unconditional.

And go, I'll wait right here till you're back.

Chapter Four

THE TIMES I ACTUALLY WROTE IN MY JOURNAL

THE ESSAYS

Now that you've had your break, I figured it was a good time to change the pace of this book for a few chapters. These next few pages will be a little different. These essays were written on nights that were significant in my journey of overcoming my own madness. Looking back over the 10+ year journey of dealing with anxiety and depression, I can say that life has taught me the value of having life changing nights. *Those* nights that could not have been written better even if John Hughes tried to touch it. They are the nights you remember for your whole life, because they were simple and beautiful. Sometimes, those moments are heartbreaking, and sometimes, they bring life. The following sections in this chapter are pages I ripped out of my journal. (That journal that I rarely wrote anything in — but somehow these days seemed to make it in.) They celebrate the moments of long-awaited friendship, mourn the loss of a small life, and reveal glimpses of eternity when we will all be home. These are stories of when my madness found freedom and when it taught me this world is not my home. If you're lucky, sometimes those nights are filled with a really good Bruce Springsteen song.

BRUCE SPRINGSTEEN
SAVED MY NIGHT

(Photo evidence that this actually happened.)

Saturday, November 9th, 2013

We drove a caravan from Los Angeles to a small house right outside the city of Palm Springs for a long weekend. The following week would be my 22nd birthday. The travel was easy, and I think everyone was ready for a little time away from the bustle of Los Angles. We made it to the strip of Palm Springs by dinner, and walked along the deserted sidewalks for most of the night. We bumped into a few strangers on the street who were crowded around a small tavern. It was loud, but we dismissed it as a noisy bar. Tommy looked over the heads of a few of patrons outside and heard the drunken melodies of customers inside.

A karaoke bar.

Indulging in what might be fun to watch a few intoxicated crooners, we stepped inside and slowly slipped to the front right of the room next to the bar. Beatriz grabbed the attention of the bartender and asked to see the song catalog. I distanced myself as much as possible, because there was no way I wanted to participate in a Destiny Child trio. Leslie joined Beatriz and the two walked to the other side of the bar to choose a song. It had been a long dream of Leslie's to do karaoke.

I saw an open seat at the bar next to an older gentleman and made my way over to watch some guy dedicate his next number to Sinatra and his wife standing in the corner.

"Would you go up there if I do a song?" Tommy asked.

"What?" I replied.

Leslie and Beatriz told the bartender they had made their selection, "Irreplaceable" by Beyonce, and I guess that meant we were going to stick around for a while. We stuck around for every Top 40 song from the past forty years to be covered nearly twice, waiting for Leslie and Beatriz's names to flash on the screen to get ready. While we were waiting, a group of middle-aged mothers asked Tommy if he was going to sing. Tommy coyly dodged their encouragement and made a few jokes about needing a few more drinks. With how much they questioned him, I'm surprised they didn't open a tab for him and pay for every one.

"What about a Bruce Springsteen song?" he asked me.

"Um, okay," I answered. I wished to take those words back. I didn't even have a drink; I was in complete control of my words and still agreed. Must be something in the karaoke air of Palm Springs.

Tommy turned to his fans and informed them he was going to put his name in to sing. They asked what he was going to sing and he responded,

"Bruce."

When contemplating song choices for karaoke — debating if Bruce Springsteen is a good song choice is not even a fair debate to have with yourself. It is no contest that he is an excellent choice for the first time up to bat. The moms loved it too.

My stomach turned in knots over the 45-minute wait we had until we performed. As each performer left the stage, I considered turning to Tommy and telling him I was going to sit this one out. What am I doing here? We aren't these people.

Are we these people? Are we the kind of kids that stand around a karaoke bar with a bunch of middle-aged to retired folks and sing Top 40 from 1983?

Our names rolled across the screen to be prepared to go after the current performer, and I couldn't feel my arms. Andrew and Steve ran into the back of the room just in time to grab quick hugs and pull out their phones to record what could be the biggest embarrassment of our lives.

We held our microphones as the first few notes of *Dancing in the Dark* roared through the monitor.

"Were they even alive during this song?" a super fan of our work yelled to his buddy across the table.

We most certainly were not.

"I was born in 1991," I mumbled into my microphone that had yet to be turned on. Thank God.

Tommy gripped his hand on top of the microphone and grumbled the first few lines of the song. Very Bruce of him. He leaned with the microphone stand towards the table in front of the small stage, belted the bridge, and seamlessly wooed the middle aged couples finishing their third round of beers. I was his hype-man, and sometimes if I remembered I would sing the chorus.

By the time the chorus kicked on, the crowd sang along to every note. Tommy shot a glance towards the moms who were waving their drinks in the air and singing along like the Boss was on-stage himself. He put every ounce of showmanship into that song and the crowd loved him for it. Andrew was standing in the back with a wide smile smacked across his face the entire three minute set. If you've never sung your heart out to a Bruce Springsteen song in karaoke, you haven't lived yet.

Andrew rushed up to us to give us the biggest hug. He was floored.

"That was like a scene from a movie!" He thumbed through a couple of pictures on his phone and laughed in awe at our little performance. We caught the moms on our way out who were having one more drink. They loved every minute.

We disappeared into the night and ran down the empty sidewalks to our cars. Andrew jumped into the passenger seat of my Malibu and threw in our tunnel songs playlist. It's important to have a CD kept in the car at all times for night drives with good people in big cities. We drove down the vacant streets to The Killer's newest single, "Shot in the Night." Andrew rolled down his window and shoved his long, blonde hair outside. We saw a white Jeep appear in the review mirror and make its way into the lane next to us. Tommy threw his head out of the window of the white, Jeep. Andrew turned the radio louder as the chorus bounced off the cement walls and echoed throughout the whole dimly lit tunnel. For a few moments we drove through our own personal amphitheater.

This is what it felt like to be young. The good kind of young that makes you want to keep living. As we raced into a growing black hole, I experienced a glimpse of eternity. Forever feels like this. It's hard to image getting old and soon enough these stories turn into old memories that we may or may not remember when we are wrinkling. This was the time to be young, because we were never going to be young again. For the first time in my life I gave myself the permission to feel, the permission to be young, the permission to heal, and the permission embrace a moment of freedom. We breached the end of the tunnel and a gust of wind hit our faces. We were free from the madness, if only for a moment.

BABY HARTUNG

May 29th, 2013

Loss is one of those things that can never be explained. It's a numbness that inhabits every working limb throughout the body while a heart-shaped ball forms in the back of the throat filled with questions, heartache, and anger. Words, which in most cases have been useful for expression, fall short to even lightly explain the hurt sitting inside. Emotions cannot become tangible for others to pick up and carry away while trying to cope with the mess left by the fall of mankind. It can be one of the darkest valleys ever walked through in this life. Loss is not a defeating battle for the weak — it is a measure of endurance.

My family is small. We are a tight-knit unit of crazy characters suitable for a crossbred pilot for a PBS special and an ABC Family show that should precede an episode of *Melissa & Joey*. We haven't done great things. We aren't written about in history books, and most people don't remember to send us Christmas cards or dinner invitations — but in my family, we like it that way. We like doing things for other people. Most don't understand us and have a hard time accepting a family that bears no motive. This quality is the one that makes me proud to be a Hartung.

This is what makes loss in a family much harder. Watching the people you love most in this world lose an important member — even if that member didn't have a chance to make their first joke, open their first Christmas gift, or breathe their first breath.

God always has a plan. I believe His plan isn't always clear, but it is always good.

Baby Hartung,

I will never have the chance to awkwardly hold you for the first time in the hospital as I did with your brother. We won't beat on pots and pans in our makeshift drum line or spend a few hours twirling around to musical soundtracks that would make Ginger Rogers and Fred Astaire green with envy. We'll never hear your little cracks of laughter as your Dad tickles your foot or listen for a faint whimper when the dark scares you. You will never grab the leg of your Mom as she walks you into your first day of kindergarten or let Grandma and Grandpa feed you something that your parents said you shouldn't eat. You also won't get to wear the *Love My Aunt* t-shirt I brought you last week.

You will miss a lot in this world, but the world that you are in now is much greater than any Disney World trip that we would take here. You will never experience a broken heart, a scary dream, or the loss of someone you love. You are safe. You are home.

You will be missed at every dinner, absent from every picture, and desired in every memory. You will never be forgotten.

We are a family — and you will *always* be a part of it.

PATTERNS & RHYTHMS

Sunday, May 18th, 2014

We sat at a table in the back of a softly lit coffee shop across from the 101 highway. As conversation flowed on about milkshakes, embarrassing technology glitches, and a handful of theological statements; Camryn, our boss from the Music & Arts team at Biola, threw a question into the mix.

"What is one of the greatest lessons you've learned this year?"

Tommy and Maddie shared stories from leadership or personal experience that became important for their journeys over the past year. I had trouble articulating a solid answer as I listened to the others.

We drove down the familiar streets under the diming lights to the static sounds of The Temptations from a distant radio station. The 5 South led us back to our university as it had done hundreds of times before. As we passed the headlights of oncoming cars, I realized this moment was my greatest life lesson: The lesson of patterns and rhythms.

Life seems to only make sense to us in familiar terms of patterns and rhythms. Much like my drive from Hollywood to La Mirada, I found security in recognizing the same streets, the same lights, the same signs, and the same people. When those patterns are removed, we panic. We feel unsafe, and naturally, anxiety assumes a fitting role in our lives. By the time I reached my bed that night, the same bed I've slept in since I moved to California, I questioned why I found such assurance in patterns. We've fallen deeply in love with patterns. That is why growing up gets so tricky. As my college career came to a close, I made the official move from a small suburb of Los Angeles to the heart of Downtown. To move away from a place so familiar is removing the current pattern and allowing for a new one to begin. New patterns are scary things. We are terrified of the unknown and lovers of repetition. As patterns change, we must adapt to the new one — but only for a short time. Life on earth is only the short version. We live under the patterns to find balance of a Savior only to one day live in a presence that has no sense of nostalgia, only sweet future.

Darkness can seem like a flow of endless patterns and rhythms. Highs and lows. There are good days and bad days. Days that seem like they will never end, and nights that will never see the break of morning. The repetition can seem cold and lonely, but they exists to make safe of the unknown. The more we tap into the patterns of our madness, the more we can find safety. Stigma has deterred us away from taking the time to understand our minds, and instead offered sweeping stereotypes.

We must fight to find safety.

Find safety in the patterns of good friends who sit up with you on the hard nights, find patterns in the rhythms and sounds of your favorite Earth, Wind, and Fire song (Mine is *September*, if you wanted to know) and allow grace to cradle you in the times you cannot find the pattern you need. Learning to deal with my depression was a matter of taking captive the patterns it had on my life, and making space for new ones. I believe we can share in our experiences. I choose to not look at my depression as an impossible hurdle but as a rare door that opens my eyes to see and understand people. We are not broken, but fully alive when we do life together.

Chapter Five

ONE LAST THING

COMING FULL CIRCLE

'm a sucker for stories that come full circle. It doesn't matter how terrible a movie storyline is or how awful a television sitcom runs, if there is an *ah-ha!* full circle kind of story — I'm into it. So, now that we've come to our last chapter together, (I told you it wouldn't take that long. You're probably nearing the end of your flight) I wanted to end this story with a small full circle moment.

I was nearing my college graduation and decided to take a summer to teach improv class at a children's home in Bellflower, California. Comedy had become so instrumental in my own healing and understanding the story I was given. In what was a very enthusiastic attempt to bring healing into the lives of others, was in return, a lesson of friendship, change, and the power of the human story. The next two stories were written after the days I finished teaching and rushed over to a small coffee shop by my house and scribbled everything down.

LIFE LESSON OF TEACHING IMPROV: PART ONE

s that your natural hair color?" a scruffy, blonde-haired, blue-eyed boy posed as I entered the room. His eyes were covered by chunks of thick, unwashed hair, normal for a 14-year-old boy that toted a skateboard under his arm. He brushed his hair away from his forehead by throwing his neck back, flinging the locks behind his oversized ears.

"I'm more of a redhead," I replied.

"A redhead! Oh man, why didn't you keep that? Redheads are the best!" he said. His question was followed by additional questions: *Where do you go to college? Are you from Los Angeles? Are you even funny?* I tried to answer, but by the time I started to speak he was already preoccupied with other conversations with the kid next to him. Damien had resorted to using his

Batman voice to get the attention of little Maya who was sitting in the corner.

"Your name is Brooke, right?" Jacob asked. He was full of questions.

"No, I'm Maya and today is my birthday," She smiled.

"Happy birthday, Maya. Has anyone sang 'Happy Birthday' to you today?" I asked.

"No." She resisted the impending attention, but a smirk escaped out of the right side of her mouth that secretly welcomes the song because it really is nice to hear someone sing to you on your birthday.

We sang, off-key. Juan and David, the other leaders, led the baritone section in our a cappella orchestra. Kevin, a 16-year-old thin kid with worn-out Converse and a dirty yellow shirt walked in on the last bar of the song. He announced to the group, sitting in a semi-circle, that he was an alcoholic for the past 20 years and he was here for his first AA meeting. The kids laughed. The baby of the group, Matthew, looked up from under his long brown hair and yelled, "This is improv class!" And that was the first day of teaching improv that summer at a home for foster kids and those waiting to be adopted.

I didn't come to work with the "underprivileged youth" out of cultural conviction. I was adopted — I understood. I understood what it's like to joke that you have no friends when in reality all you really are is telling the truth. Comedy eventually helped me in my healing, and I was only there to pass on the few tips I had gathered in the past six years. As one of them. Jacob kept asking if he would make friends by the end of the class. He would smile, but a glisten of despair run away from his eyes. That's the toughest part of being a kid — never feeling wanted. It broke my heart to know that Jacob didn't have a Mom to tell him she loved him tonight.

They were already halfway through their improv scenes when I snapped back into the moment. Loud and obnoxious, we struggled to work our way through exercises and warm-ups. They hardly listened to anything any of the leaders said and Kevin decided to dance around the rule, "No dirty words." He made drug references that, as a 22-year-old, I still don't understand. David pulled him aside into another room of the facility, and we tried to fill the silence with more sketches. Kevin re-emerged, with a cleaner mouth, and the hour-long class was done.

The kids ran into the other room when we informed them of the awaiting pizza. "Do you ever lose your humor?" Kevin asked me as I walked around the corner of the room. "I guess. Sometimes I'm really insecure," I said. "I have all these thoughts…" he paused, holding on to his words before he stated them. A really smart guy. "…thoughts and feelings in my head, and I heard humor is good to get them out. Do you know psychology at all?"

"Yeah." I quickly wrestled with spilling out every academic journal of humor research I had learned over the past two semesters of college, or I could just listen. I chose to listen, because sometimes that's all you need to do. I bit my lip. He continued, "It's like smoking marijuana with your friends and laughing, huh? It makes you close. It makes you brothers." My mind raced to think about how Kevin was spending his time outside of class.

"Kind of," I responded. "Laughing makes you brothers."

Kevin become more respectful as the next few minutes rolled in, a sense of maturity hit him when he carried on conversation with the fellow leaders in the room. Carlos, a new intern, watched from the side of the room, eating his pizza and possibly a little shell shocked from the past hour of inappropriate jokes and wild junior highers. Kevin declined the extra pizza on the table. David hollered for the kids to head to the van and grabbed the empty pizza boxes. Kevin fought an unknown origin of emotion and leaned his back against the wall. "Take the pizza, Kevin. Wrap it up and put it in your pocket," I said shoving the last pizza box his way. He smiled, "There's nothing like cold Little Caesars in an hour." He grabbed a piece. "You're 16, what are you doing? Take two." I pushed the box closer. "I'll see you next week!" he shouted as he ran to the van.

I drove to a coffee shop a few blocks from my house to write down their story. I realized in the matter of two hours, eight snotty-nosed punks changed my life. I received an e-mail from David that read of Maya's deep appreciation for being sung to today. She had no one else to sing to her. It's cliché to say that it only takes a few moments for someone to change your life. It's true. We are a brotherhood. Maybe that's the problem with change: we long too much about changing the lives of others, when really they are changing ours. Even the least of these.

I came home and tossed some mail and trash into our bin. I picked up the box of hair dye and tossed it in, too.

LIFE LESSON OF TEACHING IMPROV: PART TWO

C an I ask you a question?" Kevin asked.

"Go for it," I replied as I finished shaping the black chairs into a half-circle across our makeshift stage.

"Have you ever met somebody who had a lot in common with you?" Kevin stumbled over his words and apologized for his scattered thought. "I'm sorry. Does that make sense?"

"Yeah, and yes. I have met friends who I have a lot in common with," I said while the faces of the handful of friends I've accumulated over my short 22 years of life raced into my mind.

"Do you still talk to them?" he pressed, slowly, his words dripped with hopeful optimism.

"Some of them. Some I've grown apart from and the ones that have stayed, I may only see for a few hours each week; but I'm learning to cherish those hours," I answered.

Damarion entered the room and I patted his shoulder as he sat in a chair two seats away from Kevin. Blake trickled in a few moments later with his Dr. Dre headphones resting around his neck and an iPhone sticking out of his pocket. He turned to David and told him of an audition he had later today. He was really excited for it because he really wanted to act one day.

"Do you think it was college? Was it college that pulled you apart, I mean?" Kevin didn't seem to mind the other kids hearing his delicate questions. The voices overlapped in various conversations, but he was determined to have his questions answered.

"No, well maybe," I misunderstood the question.

"It's just tough when they talk bad about you behind your back," He sighed and followed with a quirky laugh to cover up any sadness that might have penetrated that last comment. "You know?"

I froze. Completely accepting the fact that I did know. I knew very much the life that Kevin was living, but had no means of sharing my life story in the next two minutes before our improv class started. I gave him a reassuring nod and bumped into Jacob as he walked in the room. I realized Jacob was the 15 year old skater version of my friend, Andrew. Also a shaggy haired blonde kid with a sweet, sweet spirit. Jacob is a good one. So is Andrew.

We blazed through scenes and sketches like they had been doing them for three weeks. Which they have. We were now in the middle of our camp and my heart has grown so full over each one of these kids. I really do believe there is something beautiful about laughter. If only for a mere moment we are taken away by the troubles of this world and are given a glimpse of a perfect eternity. As they performed scenes with partners the world spun slower, in an unconcerned movement of a few simple moments, and all I could hear was the laughter. I could tell they were proud that they could make each other laugh. I was proud too.

Kevin always seemed to catch where I was sitting by the time the class was over and everyone had gone outside for pizza. At this point of classes, I expected his lines of polite interrogation and sat in places that had plenty of seats around my own. He continued the conversation we started earlier in the day.

"Do you think we look alike?" He held up a picture of a girl that he had befriended over the past few years.

"A little," Jacob chimed in.

"I guess," I offered.

"We are like the same person, but her boyfriend doesn't like me and she talks really bad about me behind my back. I feel like I'm doing a lot for her, but she doesn't really return anything." Kevin apologized for stumbling over his words again. "It's tough when people don't like you.

It is tough. The thought raced through my mind as I prayed for a simple expression of wisdom in this tender moment. "A professor told me once that there is no bad book merely only books that are needed for different seasons of our lives. If we pick up a book, and we don't understand it, we shouldn't feel obligated to finish reading it. There are thousands of books available that we could read and interpret at this season of life. Perhaps one day, we will be able to pick up those books that we didn't understand at first and read them with joy and satisfaction. Maybe people are a little like books. When people don't like us, and we can't understand why it hurts so much, maybe we need to put them on the bookshelf and dust them off when our lives cross paths again. Respect all, but stay close with people who you can understand and more importantly, people who you can love well." I looked to Jacob and Kevin to see if my gust of air made any sense at all. Usually, I have to verbally process these things with people and this was a relatively premature thought for me.

Kevin nodded.

"The tough ones make you realize how sweet the good friends are, you know?" I followed.

"Yeah. They do," Kevin replied.

"Keep people in your life that let you call at 3 in the morning because you're crazy and you need someone to talk with for a few minutes or hours or days. Do the same for them. I think that's friendship."

"Always answering the phone, huh?" Kevin asked. "Do you have people like that?"

Those faces flashed through my mind one more time. Faithful faces who have constructed a patchwork family filled with brokenness, creativity, night drives to abandoned beaches, good songs at wedding receptions, picnics on top of Los Angeles, and sitting o-top of cars as the sun sets behind the rocks of Joshua Tree.

ONE LAST THING

We've almost made it. Just a few pages left before we say goodbye. I wanted to let you know I really appreciate you taking the time to buy this book, and I want to give a bigger thank you to those who have made it to the end. I am often asked in interviews, *what is the book about?* Now that you've read it, you may be able to answer that question: *Oh, just some girl who cries too much at Lifetime movies!* That is (sadly) 100% correct, but I also hope this story — in all its madness — reflects your story. My desire for you is to walk away from this book and know that your story is important. You are no mere coincidence or hiccup placed at random in the world. You were born in the right decade, at the right moment, for an extraordinary reason. As your life shifts and changes, you have the beauty of discovering the story of you. The story is wrapped up in humility and packaged to the community in order to inspire and offer hope to others who haven't been able to find their own voice. That is why I wrote this book, and I hope that is why you share your story, too.

There is an important note to make about this idea of story. In order to keep the romance of it all at bay, I will say this: Your story will continue. For those who feel stuck and cannot imagine a day when it will be different — your story will continue. For those who believe you have arrived to the top of the mountain — your story will continue.

I remember sitting in the garage of Tommy's house, a few weeks before we graduated from college. Tommy is a lover of knowledge. He is always in constant search of a good book and stimulating conversation. As we often shared our anxieties with each other, that night was no different when he began to question what post-grad life might look like for us.

"How do we learn after college?"

He raised a valid point. We had only known a world set up by an education system. We hadn't experienced learning without homework or teachers since we sat on our living room floor with our parents coaching us on animal sounds. I didn't answer in the moment and allowed space for the rhetorical comment to float around our heads for a bit. Throughout the last few days of school, I kept the question in the back of my mind. I thought about the first time I stepped onto my college campus as an eager transfer student with all the worldviews I had cultivated and a firm grip on everything I thought to be true. Then I walked across the stage, a completely different human being. What was the reason for the change? Sure, I took some great classes and found some great mentors. There were good books that I (sometimes) read for homework, and smart speakers who showed up for our weekly chapels. The real change, however, was listening to a world of stories saturated in hope.

To understand story is to understand a world beyond the four walls of an academic institution and embrace the adventure of other worlds, languages, and cultures. We must listen to the stories of others, and be brave to contribute our own. There is significance and power in the story of us. We learn to fight for those whose voices have gone numb from shouting so loud into an empty chasm. We're humbled by those who are unlike us and have given so much to a world that never gives them anything in return. We embrace the ones that we do not understand, and we surrender to the love that has been built into the story of humanity.

One more thing I want to make sure you have sealed in the inner lining of your soul before you set this book on your shelf and it collects dust until your next garage sale: We are not alone. Slow down, take a deep breathe, and take a moment to think about the faces of those who have crossed your path over the course of your life. Remember the laughter, the tears, the late-night donut runs, the births, the deaths, the wedding receptions that you danced to "Come on Eileen," the nights you forgot your medication, and the mornings that faith woke you up to, and remember — remember this forever — we are the story of humanity. We're all just sort of running in the dark. (Did you see what I did there?)

We'll talk again real soon.

REFERENCES

Brown, Brené. *Daring Greatly: How the Courage to Be Vulnerable Transforms the Way We Live, Love, Parent, and Lead.* New York, NY: Penguin Group (USA), 2012.

Buechner, Frederick. *Telling Secrets.* New York: HarperCollins e—books, 2007.

Fey, Tina. *Bossypants.* New York: Back Bay Books/Little, Brown, 2012.

Hatfield, Elaine, Richard L. Rapson, and John T. Cacioppo. *Emotional Contagion.* Cambridge University Press, 1993.

Kerouac, Jack. *On the Road.* Reprint. Penguin Publishing Group, 1976.

Kleinbaum, N. H. *'Dead Poet's Society'.* New York: Hyperion, 1989.

Lynch, O. H. 'Humorous Communication: Finding a Place for Humor in Communication Research.' *Communication Theory* 12, no. 4 (2002): 423—45. doi:10.1093/ct/12.4.423.

Schwartz, Sherwood. 'The Brady Bunch', ABC Television, 1969.

9 781630 475079